1945←2015

Reflections on Stolen Youth

Yuriko Ochiai   Naomi Kitagawa   Motomi Murota

Translation by Deborah Iwabuchi

Korocolor Publishers

Interviews conducted and compiled
Motomi Murota
Naomi Kitagawa

Photographs
Yuriko Ochiai

Translation
Deborah Iwabuchi

Japanese version editing
Naomi Kitagawa

English version editing
Stephanie Umeda

Book Design
Manami Yasuda
Jun Ando

The First Edition 2020

Korocolor Publishers
Aoi Bldg. 603, 1-19-7 Akabane, Kita-ku, Tokyo, Japan
Tel. +81(0)3-5939-7950
office@korocolor.com

ISBN 978-4-907239-51-0

Asia Pacific War of the Fifteen Survivors

This map shows the location of the survivors during the war

Russia

Mongolia

Harbin ○ ● **Yoshio Shinozuka**
Pingfang

● Changchun
Nobuko Yamatani

○ Fushun

China

Beijing ○   Dalian ○   *North Korea*

South Korea

Japan

Nagano   ○ Fukushima

Laiwu ●   ● Tokyo
Yasuji Kaneko

Hiroshima   **Michiko Kiyo-oka**

Luoyang ●   Osaka ○   **Fusako Iwase**

Nagasaki

Masaji Shinagawa

Shanghai   ○ Shanghai

Hiroko Iwami

Main Island   **Sanae Ikeda**
of Okinawa

Shisono Hisamatsu

Hateruma   *Taiwan*
● Island

Taeko Shimabukuro

Koyu Kinjo   **Michiko Miyagi**

Myanmar

Laos

Zenko Nakasoko

Thailand

Hintok   *Vietnam*   *Philippines*

● Bangkok ○

Cambodia

Lee Hak Rae

Malaysia

Singapore   *Indonesia*

Morimichi Tsukahara

Hollandia ●   ○ Wewak

*Papua
New Guinea*

Australia

Contents

Foreword

Motomi Murota

You might be wondering what 1945←2015 means. 1945 is the year the Asia Pacific War (World War II) ended. More than three million Japanese and twenty million people throughout Asia died in that war. This book contains the stories of fifteen people who lived through it as young people. We then asked fifteen youth of today (2015) to read the stories and write letters to the survivors. This was our way of transcending generations to get youth—young and old—to reflect together on war and peace.

We three who took the photographs, did the interviews, and compiled the stories and letters, are part of the Japanese generation that has not experienced war. We had heard a little about those years from our parents, but about ten years ago we realized that if we didn't make an effort to meet war survivors now, we might completely miss our chance. We began to go around the country, meeting and talking with, and taking the portraits of, those who had lived through the war when they were young.

Most people know about the atomic bombs dropped on Hiroshima and Nagasaki, but many of the other stories recounted in this book were situations that not even Japanese people know about. We met a former soldier who expressed deep remorse for killing Chinese people during the war, and a mother in Manchuria who had to give up her baby if either of them was going to have a chance of escape during the post-war chaos. There were many young people who were forced into fighting in the Battle of Okinawa. Then there was a Korean man involved in the war only because the Japanese had colonized his country. After the war he lost his Japanese citizenship but was still convicted and sentenced to death as a Japanese war criminal.

The one thing these fifteen survivors had in common was that they were young during the war. Some said that the war stole their youth. As they told us their stories, some cried out of sadness and regret. Indeed these young people lost far more than their youth: also stolen were their parents, brothers and sisters, and friends; not to mention their homes, fortunes, dreams for the future, and sense of identity as a unique individual. War took from them far more than we can imagine.

We, the photographer and authors, decided that we wanted the young people who will be leading our society in the near future to know more about the war. How would modern-day young people receive these stories of youth who had made it through the war? What are they thinking about life in general?

To find out, we asked fifteen young people of today to read the survivors' testimonies and write down their impressions as letters to them. We even asked for input from Asian young people whose countries had been victims of the Japanese war. To tell you the truth, we were afraid our young readers wouldn't be interested in the war and perhaps have no desire to write letters. Imagine our surprise when we got more interest than we could incorporate into a single book.

And so this book came to be: youth born in completely different eras transcending time to come together on the page to discuss peace.

In 2019, we finally completed the English translation of this book with the aim of sending it out to people around the world. Our hope now is to transcend space to have people in different countries read the stories and letters. How can we get rid of war on a planet that is never free of armed conflict? What should we do in the midst of a world in chaos? It is our fervent hope that people throughout the world who read the stories of the fifteen war survivors and the letters of the fifteen young people of today will come together to talk about peace.

Michiko Kiyo-oka
1923–2017

Victim of the Tokyo Air Raids

"It has been a wound in my heart all this time: I survived, but lost my father and elder sister."

In the final days of the Asia-Pacific War, about 120 cities in Japan were hit by U.S. air raids. There was much damage and many lives were lost. Tokyo suffered about one hundred attacks in all, but the bombings in the early hours of March 10, 1945 are referred to as the Tokyo Air Raids. About three hundred B-29s flew over Tokyo, randomly dropping bombs over a period of two and a half hours. The downtown area was turned into a wasteland. More than one million people were injured and one hundred thousand were killed. Streets and rivers were filled with the bodies of victims. Michiko Kiyo-oka grew up in Tokyo's Asakusa district and spent many happy childhood days playing in the Sumida River. On March 10, the year she was twenty-one, that special place turned into the scene of a horrible disaster.

My home was right behind Asakusa's statue of Kannon, the goddess of mercy. There were always lots of people there, just like having a festival every day of the year. My father was an entertainer in a music hall, and my elder sister taught and sang traditional ballads.

By the end of 1944, though, air raids were taking place at all times of the night and day, and the music halls and movie theaters were closed. We suffered from a lack of sleep because the sirens woke us up almost every night.

One day a neighbor working at the post office joked, "Oh, I wish I could go to America and get a good night's sleep!" I laughed along with the other neighbors, but then we hurried back home because we knew there'd be trouble if the military police overheard us. Still, even during those grim years, the people of Asakusa had a sense of humor and said silly things like that.

March 1945 was so cold that buckets of water for putting out fires would freeze. The day of the great air raids was cold and windy, too. Before bed, my elder sister and I pulled out our futons and lined them up next to each other. We talked about how it would be awful if there were air raids that night, and then we climbed in and went to sleep. A warning siren sounded once before midnight, but then it was quiet for a while. It was just after 12 a.m. when the air-raid siren suddenly blasted.

My father was in charge of getting people in the neighborhood evacuated, so he was the first up, calling out, "Incendiary bombs!" I followed him outside. The sky was full of more huge airplanes than I'd ever seen before. They looked like a swarm of humming dragonflies, flying slowly and very low, dropping bombs everywhere. It was terrifying.

The house across the street was hit and burst into flames. My father, fearing for the worst, called out, "We've got to escape to Sumida Park!" My parents, sister, and I clung to each other and ran off toward the Sumida River. Unfortunately we were downwind. We all wore iron helmets and air-raid hoods, and had rucksacks on our backs. We used both arms to carry our bedding. If we lost our futons, we'd never be able to replace them.

We made it to Sumida Park, but we were still in danger of getting hit by a bomb. We took shelter under Kototoi Bridge and finally had a place to put our things down. At first there were only sparks flying through the air, but then flames were at the riverbanks. Just like a flamethrower, the fire blew under the bridge. The wind carried it like a dragon. Whoosh! The flames came licking. Anyone in the way would be burned to a crisp.

My father ordered us to jump into the river. I grabbed my mother's hand and headed for the stone staircase down to the boat landing. I was pulled into a huge wave of people and pushed from behind. When I got to the bottom step, I stopped and clung to it for dear life. I was lucky because where the stairs ended was a fishing pier that was hidden under water, and I was able to perch on it.

The night was black, and I had no idea where the rest of my family was. I found out later that my father and mother had made it to a place a little higher and closer to the riverbank and stood with their backs to the stone wall there. My sister swam to a mooring pile a little farther out in the river and held onto it. She was up to her chest in water. It was the worst place to be. On top of that, my sister was small and thin and easily chilled.

The water in the river was so cold. It was freezing. Before long I was chilled through and became numb. But the flames were close, so I just kept scooping up water with my helmet and pouring it over myself. Finally I couldn't lift my arms anymore and my mind got foggy. I remember thinking I'd die before long and that maybe this wasn't such a terrible way to go.

Kototoi Bridge on my left looked like an arch of fire. At the top of it, I found out later, people had collided as they tried to escape in both directions, from the Asakusa and the Mukojima sides. Many people died because they couldn't move forward or go back. I couldn't make out anyone because the whole bridge was in flames.

The amazing thing is that I have no memory of sound at all. I'm sure there were sounds of wind and flames and people screaming. All I remember is what it smelled like. The bombing stopped and the flames continued. Then there was just smoke. It was a thick smoke, so thick I couldn't open my eyes. There was a strong smell, too, like sardines being grilled. It was years after the war ended before I could eat sardines again.

As morning came and it got light enough to see, I climbed out of the river. I was sure I'd freeze to death if I stayed in any longer. I was wearing an overcoat, but I was cold and soaked to the skin. I saw a fire under the bridge, so I went over to it to warm myself. When I looked closer, I realized it was a human being. Someone who'd gotten caught in the flames was burning there.

After a little while I went looking for my parents and sister. The steps up from the river were covered with people who had climbed out of the water and collapsed. I couldn't tell if they were dead or alive, but I checked them all. People were burned in different ways. Some were completely burned into black lumps, while others were half-burnt, their skin blackened and peeling off. Some had climbed into steel drums and died standing in them. Of course I couldn't tell if the people were male or female. I don't think I was scared; I was past that. There were dead bodies everywhere.

At last, I found my mother. She was at the top of the stone stairs, soaking wet and unconscious. A man carried her over to where there was a fire, laid her down on the ground, and covered her with a burned futon he'd found. I never learned his name, but he saved my mother's life. There were many people that helped us over the next few days. Some gave the two of us a place to stay. Then there was the man who brought a fire hook to pull my mother out of the river in the first place. We owe those people our lives. Without them we never would have been able to cross the line back from death. Even at a time like that, there were people who stopped to help others.

When my mother regained consciousness, I left her there to sleep and went to search for my father and sister. My mother told me they might be gone for good. At about dawn, my father had told my mother to get out of the river. She said he had grabbed on to a barrel and said he was going to swim out to rescue my sister, but he didn't have the strength to go very far before she saw him go belly up.

I couldn't find my father or my sister. It wasn't until three days after the air raids that I found their bodies. My uncle came to Tokyo from Funabashi, in Chiba. He and my mother and I went to a makeshift gravesite in Sumida Park. We found markers with my father's and sister's names on them. Tin sheets had been laid over their bodies and dirt sprinkled on top of that. We uncovered them to make sure there was no mistake, and they both sprayed blood from their noses. It was just like the saying, "Dead bodies bleed from their noses when their family finds them."

Up till then, all I could think of was finding my father and sister, but now there was nothing to keep me going. I broke down and cried and cried. I couldn't stop the tears. Everything had been lost in the air raids. We didn't have a place to live or food to eat. I was the younger child in the family and had grown up spoiled, but I realized that without my father or sister, it would be my job to take care of my mother, who was frail. There was no more time for crying. I knew I had to deal with whatever came my way. It was the last time I ever shed tears.

I was haunted in my sleep with dreams of my father and sister. I had managed to help my mother, but not them. It has been a heavy burden to bear. I wasn't far—I should have been able to hear them. If I'd tried harder, surely I could have found them. I'll never get over that sorrow. I still wonder why I was the one who survived. It has been a wound in my heart all this time.

It's only in the last few years that I've been able to talk about what happened that night. I was even a plaintiff in the trial.[1] The national government rejected our plea. It was the same as saying all of those lives weren't really lost in that one night of air raids. Men in the military were buried with dignity, and their families received compensation, but we private citizens received neither an apology nor payment of any kind. I hate the way they tell us it's our duty to put up with all that sorrow.

I've never forgotten about the people who died in the air raids. Not for a single day. Every morning I sit in front of the family altar and tell my father and sister, "I'm living my life for you, too."

---

[1] About 130 people injured in the air raids as well as survivors of those who died sued the national government, saying it was unfair that survivors of dead soldiers were compensated, but private citizens who incurred damages in the air raids got nothing. In May 2013 the Japanese Supreme Court ruled for the government, turning down all appeals from the injured and survivors. The government cited the "endurance doctrine," that claims "all members of the nation are obligated to equally accept and endure some loss as a result of war."

Michiko Kiyo-oka Timeline

1923
Michiko is born on November 12 in Nagano Prefecture, where her parents evacuated after the Great Kanto Earthquake on September 1 of that year. Following her birth, the family return to the Asakusa district of Tokyo.

1940
At the age of 16, Michiko graduates from Tokyo Girls' Commercial High School and begins work for the Tokyo Metropolitan Government.

1941
Michiko, aged 18.
December: Japan invades the Malay Peninsula and attacks Pearl Harbor in Hawaii, beginning the Asia Pacific War.

1944
Michiko, aged 21. The US begins B-29 air raids on Tokyo, which eventually number more than one hundred.

1945
On March 10 when Michiko is 21 years old, her father and sister are killed in the air raids (code-named Operation Meetinghouse).
In May Michiko and her mother evacuate to Nagano Prefecture.
On August 15 Japan surrenders, ending the war.

1946
Michiko, aged 22, goes back to work for the Tokyo government, with the Economic Planning Bureau, supporting her family as a Japanese-language typist. Michiko marries and has two children.

1975
At age 52, Michiko retires to care for her mother.

2001
When Michiko turns 77, she begins to actively tell others about her wartime experiences.

2006 to 2013
From the ages of 82 through 89 Michiko is a claimant in the lawsuit seeking compensation for victims of Tokyo Air Raids.

January 5, 2017
Michiko dies at the age of 93.

Dear Mrs. Kiyo-oka,

My name is Shoko Aizawa. I was born and raised in Hiroshima and had spent my entire life there until two and a half years ago when I got married and moved to Tokyo. Once here, I started working for a company, and my husband and I enjoy a rather peaceful life.

To tell you the truth, the title of your testimony made me feel nervous about reading it all. It left me wondering just how sad and painful a memory it must be. As someone who's lived her entire life in a war-free environment, I couldn't begin to imagine what it must have been like to be a civilian caught in a war. I honestly did not know how I would be able to write to you, Mrs. Kiyo-oka, someone who has survived such a tragic past.

Your testimony, however, has helped me reflect on the bombing of Tokyo, this same Tokyo where I live today. My thoughts go out to those who lost their lives and those who survived such a traumatic time. I have you to thank for this opportunity. Your memories are, without a doubt, exceptionally painful, and it must have taken an incredible strength to recollect the events and narrate them. Even though it has only been a few years since you found that strength, you made your testimony public and joined a lawsuit. Your courage and determination in taking such actions inspire in me the greatest respect and gratitude.

I think of you as someone with an unshakable strength. After all, at the time of the bombings, you were just twenty-one years old. Yet ever since that fateful day, you have been living with a wound so deep it could never be healed, and still managed to move forward with your life, without ever letting the world see your pain. Even more awe-inspiring is the way you decided that you would never cry again and that you would deal with whatever came your way in life. That promise you made to yourself to never cry again after losing your father and your

sister in the bombings gives us a small insight into how shocking the reality must have been and how deeply hurt you were. Still, you did not let it consume you. Instead, you went back to work, you got married, and you raised a family. To think that I, in comparison, am sometimes overwhelmed by my job and my life makes me feel quite ashamed.

I might be twenty-eight years old already, but at times, I feel like I am still a child. When I was a student, I was sheltered by my parents, and blessed to have everything I needed. Unfortunately, I never quite took the time to figure out what my dreams were, what it was that I wanted to accomplish in my lifetime. At age twenty-three, I got a job and became a contributing member of society, but I find I am still searching for my purpose in life. I know you started working when you were a mere sixteen years old, and from eighteen to twenty-one you lived the life of a civilian in the midst of a war. I can't help but wonder if you had dreams of your own back then, and if so, what were they? Do you ever stop and wonder how different life would have been if it hadn't been for the war, if Tokyo had never been bombed? It might seem insensitive of me to ask such a question to someone like you, someone who has bravely faced tragedy and yet kept a positive attitude toward life, but if there is ever an opportunity for you to respond, I would love to hear about those dreams.

Seventy years after the Tokyo Air Raids, there are unfortunately almost no remaining signs in the city of the tragedy that befell its many citizens. Asakusa has now become largely a popular tourist spot; passing on the vivid memories of the bombings will be quite a challenge. To be honest, I am guilty of a lack of awareness of this history myself, thinking that "wars and bombings" are a thing of the past. Unless I make a conscious effort, they are nothing but distant matters to me.

And that is exactly why your testimony, Mrs. Kiyo-oka, and the trial for the victims and survivors of the bombings, are so important.

Thanks to these voices of the past, thanks to your courage in coming forward to tell your story, we are all compelled to see it is also our story, our lives.

The government invoked the "endurance doctrine" in response to your testimony. According to them, it was your duty as a citizen of the nation to endure losses as a result of the war. This was so revealing of how the government thinks of its citizens, during that war and in the present as well. Speaking frankly, I find it very frustrating that this was their only answer when solicited to bring peace and justice to its deeply wounded people.

Sometimes I wonder about the future of Japan, and cases like this make me feel unsafe and unsure about it. What's important, however, is that we, the younger generation, take charge and decide on actions that need to be taken.

Mrs. Kiyo-oka, I promise to make sure that now, seventy years after the war, and into the future, your story's impact on our lives is not forgotten. For my part, whatever challenges come my way, I will recall your strength—the way you fought back those tears and faced the future—and try to show the same strength myself.

I would like to end this letter by saying that despite never meeting you in person, I feel very blessed to have had this correspondence and connection with you. I pray that each and every one of your days ahead will be filled with health, peace, and happy thoughts.

Best wishes,
Shoko Aizawa

Shoko Aizawa from Hiroshima, Japan.
Age 28, company employee in Tokyo.

Translation by Oulimata Gueye from Dakar, Senegal.
Age 27, graduate student in Tokyo.

Yasuji Kaneko
1920–2010

Sixteen Years at War — in Siberia and
in the War Crimes Center

*"It was only after I'd gotten married and
become a father that I realized just how terrible
my actions had been."*

Yasuji Kaneko was drafted into the army during the Sino-Japanese War and sent to Shandong Province in China. As a new conscript he was trained to kill, and as part of a military sweep he murdered civilians. When the war was over and he'd survived an internment camp in Siberia, rather than being sent home to Japan, he was moved to Fushun War Criminals Management Center where he was held for six years as punishment for war crimes. In 1956, eleven years after the end of World War II, Kaneko was exonerated from prosecution and sent back to Japan by way of Maizuru City on the Kouan-maru repatriation ship. In his old age Kaneko did what he could to atone for his sins by telling young people about his experiences during the war.

I was drafted on December 3, 1940, and ordered to report to Ueno Park in Tokyo. Two days before, I saw my mother and told her, "Ma, when I come back from the war, I'll be a private first class." Private first class soldiers had three stars on their collars, and the neighbors would talk about how well the son of that family had done. I thought that would make my mother happy, but she just looked at me and said, "Your ma doesn't need those sparkly pieces of sugar on your uniform. Just come back alive."

How could she say something so cruel? I thought. That was back then.

I reported to Ueno Park and boarded a ship at Shibaura bound for Shandong Province in China. We conscripts were beaten if we had dust on our uniforms or didn't answer our superiors in voices that were loud enough. I had to take care of the horses. When one of the horses refused to lift its leg for me, I punched it once in the face. A superior saw me and came running. "You son of a bitch, you hit a military horse!" he yelled and hit me five times. He told me conscripts were a dime a dozen, but it wasn't as easy to get horses.

One time, we new soldiers were taken into the woods where several Chinese farmers had been tied up. They'd probably tried to run away. We formed a line about ten meters away from them. The old guys gave us our orders. "Listen up! When I give the sign, run forward and kill the farmers!"

This was called point training, but it was really killing practice. The first soldier in line ran, then the second, then the third. I was number four. I held the tip of my bayonet out and ran forward, screaming.

It turns out there is nothing scarier than killing someone. I had been a bad boy growing up, but I was not prepared for this. My target didn't even have his eyes covered; he just stood there, tied to a tree and glaring at me. I couldn't put any power into my thrust, and my hands slipped.

My gun rammed me in the ribs and I fell backward. "You fool!" shouted the old guy, and made me do it over again. He showed me how to do it right this time. He got close to the target and moved his bayonet sideways, and the blade slipped in between the farmer's ribs. I did my level best to copy my commander, and sure enough, the blade went right in. We stabbed the farmers in the chest and stomach and killed them. That's how the military built up our courage. You can't just kill people if you think like a normal person. A year passed, and then another. Murder was no longer frightening. When a friend was killed in battle, the blood would rush to my head, and I'd just want to get back at the *chankoro* (a bad name we used for the Chinese) who'd done it.

One of my comrades was the son of a Buddhist priest. The first time we had point training, he was in tears. "I can't do it," he sobbed, and got badly beaten for it. But after a year he had no problem killing the enemy. Nobody had to tell him to. It was a terrible time.

In the fall of 1941 we were notified that the Eighth Route Army— mainly Communists—were in a village between Laiwu Province and the city of Xintai, and we attacked that village for an entire night. The next morning we started our house-to-house sweep. An older soldier and I went into one house. At first it was too dark to see inside, but when our eyes adjusted to the dim light, we saw a woman in the back holding a boy of about four. She was very still.

The older guy said to me, "Kaneko, take the brat outside. When I'm done, I'll switch with you." I took the crying boy out in front of the house and heard the woman screaming. The older soldier dragged her outside by her hair. She had tried to fight him off, and he was mad. "This bitch is out of her mind," he said, and brought her over to a deep well. "Kaneko, grab her legs," he commanded.

The two of us counted off one, two, three and threw the women into the well. The boy saw his mother fall in and ran around the well crying, "Mama! Mama!" He found something to stand on, put it up against the well, climbed up, and jumped in after his mother. It made me sick. The old guy said, "Throw in a grenade and kill them both." We'd been taught to "kill women because they bear children" and to "kill children because they grow into adults who will resist Japan."

We took all the cotton wool and wheat we found in that village. It was a huge amount. I hoped it would mean my family in Japan could eat. Kill civilians, steal food, burn down villages—we went to another country and that's what we did. If that wasn't an "invasion," what was it? I killed more than twenty people in all. I could never say this in front of my wife and kids, but I raped women, and I went to military brothels.

As soon as the war ended I was sent to a Russian POW camp in Siberia where I did five years' hard labor. We had little to eat, it was cold as hell, and the work was hard. I never knew if I'd live to see another day. I worked in mines, built houses, and cut down forests. Nothing could compare with the agony I experienced there.

My comrades died in droves from malnutrition, illness, and accidents. I'd wake up in the morning to find the guy next to me dead. I'd shake him to try to wake him up, but he'd be gone. I got used to it, and it didn't even bother me after a while. During the winter the ground was frozen and you couldn't dig a hole, so we just piled up bodies in sheds. They'd be piled up in five or six layers, just like firewood, in the same place as the brooms and other tools. Sometimes we buried the bodies in snow, but then spring would come, the snow would melt, and we'd see the bones.

Just when we thought we'd get sent home, we were moved from the camp in Siberia to Fushun War Criminals Management Center in China. I was sad; I'd worked so hard for so long, and now I was to be tried for war crimes. But we didn't kill people because we wanted to. We did it on the orders of our superiors. There is a line in the *Imperial Rescript to Soldiers and Sailors* that says, "An order from a superior is the same as an order from the Emperor, and it must be carried out immediately." We could have been put to death if we disobeyed.

At the War Criminals Management Center in China, I was interrogated and accused of having murdered civilians. "I did kill them, but I did it on orders," I insisted. The interrogator just stared at me, and said, "You may have done it on orders, but you did it!" I had nothing to say to that. It was the truth. I did it.

It was different from Siberia; we were treated well at the War Criminals Management Center. We were fed better than most Chinese and given medical treatment. But I was terrified that I would be executed. In late June of 1956, about three hundred of us were called, and we went into court. We were sure we would be put to death for our crimes. The judge read off all of our names, and at the very end said, "exonerated from prosecution." I swallowed hard. We'd been spared.

At first we were completely silent. Then the younger guys in their thirties started sobbing, then those in their forties, and finally the older men in their fifties. We'd lived through the war, through the harsh labor of Siberia, then life in the war crimes center—never knowing how much longer we'd make it. And we'd survived. We could go home. The whole group was bawling their eyes out. Even the Chinese staff broke into tears.

I asked Jin Yuan-sensei, a Chinese man who looked out for us at the War Criminals Management Center, why we'd been released.

"The Chinese are sick and tired of fighting the Japanese," he said. "We don't want to die, and that's why we're letting you go. If we execute you, the Japanese will be angry and want to go back to war with us. Let's stop war. Go back to Japan and live a rich, peaceful life." Our lives were saved by the generous policy of China.

I confessed to my crimes at the War Criminals Management Center, but it was only after I'd gotten married and become a father that I realized just how terrible my actions had been. Once, my daughter was sick and I went to see her in the hospital. When she saw me, she broke into a big smile. *What a sweet smile*, I thought. Then I remembered the little boy whose mother we'd killed and how he followed her by jumping into the well. That was when I really felt sorry for what I'd done. As my children grew up, I realized that I never wanted them to go to war. I was away for sixteen years before I came back to Japan on the repatriation ship. The ship docked at Maizuru, and from there I went back to my home in Urayasu, Chiba Prefecture. I walked into the house where I'd grown up and called out, "Ma, I'm home."

My mother was sitting next to a pot of simmering sweet beans, a dish I loved. She was blind in one eye, but she whipped around and stared into my face. Then she reached out and touched my leg. "You son of a bitch," she laughed, "you better not be a ghost!" Three months later, in mid-October, my mother died. It was almost like she was waiting for me to come home. Before she passed away, she rubbed my cheek, and I touched her breast. I realized then how much I'd missed it. It was flat as a pancake by then, but I thought about how she'd raised me on it.

I saw so many soldiers die during the war. And all of them whispered, "Ma" or "Mom" two or three times before they succumbed. Not a single one of them said, "Long live the Emperor."

Mothers are such a huge presence. I was the second oldest of five children. When I asked my ma for money, she'd hit me and tell me to go to hell; she was scary. Sadly I have forgotten my father's face, but I remember exactly what my mother looked like.

I fought for the glory of the Emperor and suffered for sixteen years, yet when I came home I faced terrible difficulties. I'd apply for a job, but when I showed them my resume, the interviewer would say, "Oh, you're back from Siberia," and that would be that, because they were afraid I might be a Communist sympathizer. *What?* I thought. *I don't get hired because I was in China?* The security police followed me around for two years after I got back. No wonder no one would employ me.

When we were soldiers we were willing to die for our country, but when we got back we were treated like criminals because we might have gotten brainwashed. It pissed me off. Our superiors had abandoned us and went home. Those of us following orders were tried as war criminals.

Soldiers are treated like trash. You tell them to kill and they have to do it—and anything else you'd like. Order them to die; they die. Soldiers have no rights. They're disposable. Human, but not human.

That's why I'm against armies; they cause great suffering for everyone. I'm going to keep on saying that war is wrong. You can prevent war without carrying guns. That's a better kind of patriotism.

Yasuji Kaneko Timeline

1920
Yasuji is born on January 28 in Chiba Prefecture.

1931
Yasuji, aged 11. The Manchurian Incident takes place.

1937
Yasuji, aged 17. The Second Sino-Japanese War begins.

1940
At the age of 20, Yasuji passes conscription inspection in April. In November, he is shipped to Northeast China after joining the army.

1941
Yasuji, aged 21.
December: Japan invades the Malay Peninsula and attacks Pearl Harbor in Hawaii, beginning the Asia Pacific War.

1942
Yasuji, aged 22. The Japanese navy suffers heavy losses in the Battle of Midway in June.

1945
Yasuji aged 25.
August 9: The Soviet Union invades Manchuria.
August 15: Yasuji is stationed in present-day North Korea when Japan surrenders.
October: Yasuji is interned in Siberia.

1950
At age 30, Yasuji is sent to China's Fushun War Criminals Management Center in July.

1956
Aged 36, Yasuji is exempted from prosecution during the war criminals trial in June, is released, and is sent back to Japan.

1957
Yasuji aged 37. The Association of Returnees from China is established.

2000
At the age of 80, Yasuji gives testimony in December about his experiences on the battlefield during the Women's International War Crimes Tribunal on Japan's Military Sexual Slavery.

November 25, 2010
Yasuji dies at the age of 90.

Dear Yasuji-san,

I'm sorry for your loss; your mother must have been very special to you. For a drafted soldier who had resigned himself to death, a mother's "just come back alive" must have been very important. You are fortunate to have even one person care so much for you.

To kill a person, to have your friends killed, to be hungry, and to see corpses piled up—all of that stole your innocence, your sense of right and wrong, leading you to kill and rape. Even now you probably cannot figure out what was an order you had to follow and what was done of your own free will. Taking action and making decisions while not being certain of your own moral compass must have been very scary. You said you weren't treated as human and were merely an expendable tool with no rights; for soldiers who weren't free to acknowledge their own humanity, expecting humility and moral judgement is cruel. A person's war experience doesn't end just because the war is over. After spending eleven years in Siberia and the War Criminals Management Center, and then to finally come home to such treatment— I think that the people who accused you of being "brainwashed" lived through the same war but didn't see its gruesomeness. The responsibility for the war does not lie only with the people in power who approved of the war and the soldiers who killed, but also on the citizens who allowed it to happen.

I studied the Nazis and the Holocaust in a university seminar. After reading what you went through, I was reminded of the survivors of concentration camps. Camps were places where obedience meant death. Among the survivors, there were those who stole bread from fellow prisoners, there were those who were guilty of murder (they were also ordered to do so). Just like you, after the war those survivors suffered enormous remorse and shame. I'm not comparing you to a Holocaust survivor or a Nazi. Suffering and wrongdoing are mixed together in any war and the result is a chaos of sorrow.

Writing this letter, I feel that I'm slowly able to see what war looks like. I can't imagine a time where the people of today, who enjoy a stable, peaceful life, are able to kill without feelings of guilt. But we should not think of that era as savage and one that can't happen again; it can. That's why it's important for people to rethink what "normal" means to them. Is violence a bad thing? Is war a bad thing? Perhaps if we keep thinking about these questions, we'll come up with a concrete definition of "normal" and fight to hold on to it. And if war ever does happen again, maybe we can keep a firmer grasp on our humanity. That's what I think. I am beginning to understand how you experienced the war. War isn't just one thing; everyone endures it, suffers through it, and witnesses it differently. I learned that from you, Kaneko-san.

Thank you,
Junpei Sekiguchi

Junpei Sekiguchi from Tokyo, Japan.
Age 22, university student in Tokyo.

Translation by Maki Miyamoto from Cavite, Philippines.
Age 24, company employee in Tokyo.

Michiko Miyagi
1926–2015

A Member of
the Zuisen Student Nursing Corps

*"I never forgot how the Japanese
discriminated against the Okinawans."*

Toward the end of the Asia Pacific War Okinawa became a battlefield, and everyone in the prefecture was mobilized. Boys in middle school, some as young as fourteen, were drafted and sent into battle. In March 1945, right before US forces landed, female students were assigned to student nursing corps attached to fighting forces and field hospitals in cave shelters. The work that awaited these young women was cruel and dangerous. Michiko Miyagi was assigned to Zuisen Corps and sent to the front lines where she was in the line of fire. More than half of her comrades died in the fighting.

I always cry on the days I visit the Zuisen Memorial in Itoman City. You all died so young, and I survived. I can still remember the faces of each and every one of my thirty-three friends who died in the war.

I'm talking about my friends now, so that as many people as possible can learn about you.

We were fourth-year students at Shuri Girls' High School, run by Okinawa Prefecture. In December 1944 we had been told to evacuate if we could, but I was a tomboy. I declared I'd never evacuate because girls should be able to work for their country as well as boys. My mother worried about me and told me not to be so quick to "stand out in front." Back in those days, I couldn't understand why my parents weren't proud of me and didn't encourage me to do my best. I was so disappointed. By March 1945 we were mobilized into the Zuisen Student Nursing Corps.

Of my 105 classmates, 61 joined the Zuisen Corps. I remember our graduation well. It was March 27. We had been under so much fire that day that we didn't get around to the ceremony until evening, when things had quieted down. A tent was put up in front of the Nagera military field hospital for the event. Guests of honor were the company commander and field doctors. The only teachers there were the two in charge of our class and the principal. We sang our school song and then belted out "If I Go Away to the Sea," a military song. Just then an American plane came flying over, and we all ran for cover in the shelter. That was the end of the ceremony.

After that we were inducted into Ishi 5325 Corps of the army's 62th Division. Our teachers told us: "Follow the instructions of your troop, and do your best for the Emperor." Then they left. The famed Himeyuri Corps of Okinawa was a troop of female students led by their teachers, but we were left all on our own.

The low-ranking army medics used us for all the dirty work. This would never happen to students today, but back then it was different. We were sent to serve soldiers meals and bring them water during battles. Refusing orders could mean death, so we just said, "Yes, sir!" and did what we were told. There was no distinction between male and female. They gave us the same abusive treatment all new army recruits were subject to.

On April 1 the first US troops landed in the middle of the west coast of the main Okinawan island. That was the beginning of the land war. We were from that area, so we were assigned to the front lines in Urasoe and Nakama. That was where Nobuko Maeshiro died. She was the first friend I lost. Nobuko was loading wounded soldiers onto a truck when shrapnel from a ship's cannon hit her in the side; she bled to death. I had ridden the train to school with her each day—in fact we train commuters had done everything together. We sang on the train, climbed the hill up to our school—always in a hurry to be first—then we made an airfield together. After she died, the rest of us knew we would be next. Now we were frightened.

With the Nakama shelter too dangerous to stay there any longer, we retreated to Nagera. Truckloads of injured were constantly coming in. There was no room to maneuver inside the shelter. When bombing became so constant that we couldn't go outside at all, we'd pee squatting inside the shelter, and the smell of blood was everywhere. I'll never forget that stench.

Finally we began to run out of food, and we could only serve meals once every three days. We ran out of medical supplies. We had loads of nothing, but the wounded kept on pouring in. There was nothing we could do for them. Their wounds were full of maggots, and their pain was unbearable. The soldiers died in droves. We were ordered to toss the dead bodies into the holes in the ground made by bombs. It was a living hell.

Still it seemed like there was medicine for people important enough. At the entrance to the shelter the military doctors asked for the rank of the wounded, sending some off to the operating room. When a soldier was announced as a member of the Okinawa Defense Force, an unofficial military organization full of local boys and older men, the physician would say, "Put 'em down," and not give them a second glance. Thinking back, it was discrimination. Even after the war was over, I never forgot how the Japanese discriminated against the Okinawans.[1]

By May the Japanese forces had lost the fight for Shuri, and we nurses were ordered to retreat to the south. We walked in threes, two girls supporting a soldier who could walk if assisted, traveling roads in the dark of night, getting drenched by rain, and always trying to avoid bombing from the battleships. We were starving, too, and the soldiers were heavy as they leaned against us. I was exhausted through and through.

On the way we rested at the Shikina shelter. Deigo Corps of the 62th Division—the same as us—was working there. An army doctor gave me an order. "Take this hypodermic needle and inject everyone on stretchers." I was squeamish about that sort of thing, so I headed toward the person in charge to ask about it. On my way I heard a voice. "Nurse, wait." The shelter was dark. The only light was from candles, so I couldn't see the face of the man. He spoke again. "I'm with the Okinawa Defense Force. I'm from Kin Village. I have a wife and baby daughter at home. If you survive, I want you to tell my family that I died here." He gave me a piece of paper with his address on it. "Mr. Soldier," I responded, "I'm on my way to Taketomi. I might die by the road or in a field. I can't deliver your message." I turned him down. And I couldn't inject the men, either. I threw away the needle and slipped out.

When I arrived at Komesu in the south, I heard a rumor. "If you had injected those soldiers, they would have died on the spot. It was poison so they could die painlessly." It was a shock to my friends and I, but by the time we realized what we'd been ordered to do and that we might be in trouble for disobeying, it was too late to go back and do anything about it.

A while after the war ended I went to Kin Village, but I couldn't find the soldier's family. It was many years later that I learned from a former member of Deigo Corps that the soldier who spoke to me had been captured the next day by US forces and had lived a long life; he only died a few years ago.

"Every year when we gathered to mourn our dead, he told us he was saved by one of the female students attached to our corps. It must have been you," recounted the Corps member.

This happened many, many years after the war was over, and I'd never told anyone about it. I was terrified to admit that I'd disobeyed orders; I could have been tried as a war criminal.

After the war, Okinawa was sold to the Americans—sold by the Japanese government. Because Japan lost the war, they were supposed to pay a huge amount of money in reparations. Instead the Emperor said, "You can take Okinawa and turn it into a military base or whatever you like."[2] That made the Americans happy; they turned Okinawa into a military base. They took the island away from us, kicked us off our land, and destroyed every trace of our lives. The stream where I played as a child, the school I went to, the fields we carried buckets of fertilizer to, the roads—everything was where Kadena Air Base is now.

You always hear about how peaceful the country has been since the end of the war. But I don't see it that way at all. We hear explosions from the base all the time. At four or five in the morning, in the middle of the night when jets take off and land. They do whatever they want. No one gives a thought for the Okinawans. There is no "post war" here.

Just remember that, even if natural disasters cannot be prevented, manmade disasters can. War is a manmade disaster. People in power make the decisions, and they might decide to go to war again. It's the citizens who bear the brunt of it. Those big guys in power don't go into battle. We all need to think about how to prevent that. Make sure you study your history. We can only move forward if we seriously reflect on the past.

---

[1] Okinawa was originally the Ryukyu Kingdom, an independent country with its own language and culture. In 1872 part of it was annexed to Japan by force. Ever since that time the Japanese have looked down on Okinawa, and even today Okinawans suffer discrimination.

[2] Memorandum entitled "Emperor of Japan's Opinion Concerning the Future of the Ryukyu Islands."
http://www.archives.pref.okinawa.jp/wp-content/uploads/Emperors-message.pdf

Michiko Miyagi Timeline

1926
Michiko is born on April 12 to a farming family on the main island of Okinawa.

1941
At age 15, Michiko begins high school.
December: Japan invades the Malay Peninsula and attacks Pearl Harbor in Hawaii, beginning the Asia Pacific War.

1944
At the age of 18, Michiko is caught in the October 10 air raid of Okinawa while on her way to school in Naha.

1945
March 27: Michiko graduates from high school and is inducted into Zuisen Corps, a corps of student nurses.
April 1: The US forces land on the main island of Okinawa.
Michiko turns 19.
May: The Zuisen Corps retreats to the southern part of the island.
June: All student corps are ordered to disband.
June 22: The Japanese army is defeated in the Battle of Okinawa.
August 15: Japan accepts the Potsdam Declaration, defining the terms for Japan's surrender.

1951
Michiko, aged 25. The Treaty of San Francisco is signed in September. Okinawa is put under the administration of the US.

1972
Michiko, aged 46. On May 15, Okinawa reverts back to Japan.

1988
At the age of 61, Michiko retires in March after 40 years teaching elementary school, and begins activities telling people about the war and promoting peace.

2010
Michiko is 84 when she brings her total number of peace lectures to over 300.

October 31, 2015
Michiko dies at the age of 89.

Dear Michiko-san,

Good evening. I am so grateful to you for sharing your memories with me. It must have been very difficult for you. I feel honored to get the chance to write you a letter. After reading your story, I feel strangely connected to you somehow.

In your testimony you wrote that you refused to be evacuated, saying, "Girls should be able to work for their country as well as boys." It was not until I read your essay that I was able to imagine how girls in the military could have been so brave. I wonder if your thoughts went something like this: "I want to be of some help. I do not want to stay behind just because I am a girl." I can understand your frustration with your parents; you wanted them to be proud when you said: "I want to try my best, so why won't they let me?" I may have felt the same way if I had been in your place.

Because you are from Okinawa, it must have stung all the more when you saw soldiers not provided medical treatment just because they were from Okinawa. Discrimination is unforgivable. The soldiers from Okinawa fought alongside those from other parts of Japan. I am mortified just thinking of how you must have felt. And I don't know what to say about the American bases being forced on Okinawa for so long. Michiko-san, what is peace for you?

How do you feel about people like me living on one of the main islands of Japan?

I read about Japan and its wartime past, but now we have Article 9 of the Constitution; we no longer have a military, and the country is at peace. I memorized the three main principles of the constitution, "national sovereignty, pacifism, and respect for fundamental human rights," when I was preparing for a test. However, looking at present-day Okinawa, do these three principles exist? The national government ignores the fact that the island population is opposed to the

US bases, and even when politicians with platforms objecting to the bases win elections, they are rarely listened to. Members of the US military repeatedly commit crimes but are not tried in Japanese courts, and now another base is to be built at Henoko. The government just makes excuses, saying it is for national security or for the economic development of Okinawa. This has gone on for seventy years! But here I am, just sitting here without a care in the world. I am embarrassed that I have paid so little attention to this issue. Now I am determined to get involved.

I think about how scared and heartbroken you must have been when you lost your precious friends. You did save that soldier by not injecting him; you could have been arrested for admitting that. You must have been so scared to talk about it even after the war.

In Okinawa last year, I walked fifty kilometers through old battle-fields, the path the student corps had walked, listening to the testimonies of people who had been there. All I was allowed were three small packages of snacks, a Calorie Mate (an energy bar), and Pocari Sweat (an energy drink). My shoes were torn and ragged, my legs were worn out, and I thought I couldn't walk another step. The meal I ate afterward was incredibly delicious. But then I realized that the student corps must have walked this path fearing for their lives. What if a fighter jet flying overhead aimed at me? Even now people in Okinawa live with the fear that jets might crash above them during daily training exercises. The constant sound of planes in the present made it uncomfortably easy to draw a direct connection to the past.

It is often said that we need armed forces for our own safety, and that Japan needs to cooperate with other countries by having military strength for "common defense." It sounds heroic, but I would like to believe that there is a way to keep people safe without resorting to war.

Michiko-san, what do you think would be a good place to start? I know this is a big question, and I haven't found a satisfactory answer yet myself. Still, there must be a way to solve the underlying problems of society without sacrificing people and resorting to violence. I hope my generation will find it.

With warm regards,
Mei

Mei Nammo from Osaka, Japan.
Age 23, university student in Kyoto.

Translation by Kasumi Furuhashi from Shizuoka, Japan.
Age 22, university student in Tokyo.

Sanae Ikeda
1933–2019

I Lost All My Brothers and Sisters in
the Nagasaki Bombing

"You can only protect peace if you stay alive."

On August 9, 1945, following the tragedy in Hiroshima, the US Army dropped another atomic bomb on Nagasaki. Sanae Ikeda was twelve years old. He survived because he had gone over the mountain to buy food. Back home afterward, he watched each of his brothers and sisters die, something no young boy should ever have to do. As the single surviving child, he had to support his parents, who could no longer work due to radiation exposure. Ikeda led a difficult life and has never gotten over losing his siblings.

That day my mother and I (then in seventh grade) had gone off to buy food from farmers on the other side of Mt. Iwaya. As we walked along the mountain path a B-29 passed overhead, and the next thing we saw was a tremendous flash of bright green light. After that came the wind from the bomb blast, and the next thing I knew, I was clinging to a big tree and my mother had fallen down in the grass. We had no idea what happened.

On our way back home we saw a cow running around with its back on fire. A military barracks was on fire, and we saw dead soldiers who had been burnt black. An old man was shouting "Water!" We could see his teeth and the whites of his eyes, but the rest of him had been badly burned. He told us a terrible bomb had been dropped and that it had destroyed Nagasaki. My mother and I found a vantage point and looked down. Sure enough the city was gone. We made our way home to Nishimachi (now Erimachi) to find that our house had been reduced to rubble.

I was the eldest son of six siblings. I had an elder sister who was fourteen, and little brothers and sisters aged ten, eight, six, and three. My father had managed to find two tatami mats, and he'd gathered all the children on them. My six-year-old sister Suzuko, though, was missing. My elder sister said, "Suzuko was out of the house when it happened." I went to look for her.

I saw a ditch full of dead people. Among them was a child who seemed about the right size. Her entire body was burned black, and her face was gone. My sister had told me that Suzuko was wearing nothing put a pair of underwear with a red flower pattern. I checked under the elastic band of what was left of the burned clothing of the child and saw two or three tiny red flowers; that was all that was left of the pattern.

I picked up my sister and carried her home, crying all the way. How could such a terrible bomb have been dropped? When night fell it was pitch black, but we heard sobbing from all directions. At first the sound was loud, but by morning it was quiet; most of the people were dead.

I heard the whistle of the rescue train arriving, and I took my three-year-old brother Saburo to meet it. Saburo's hip bones had been crushed when the columns of our house collapsed on top of him.

Knowing they'd be taken to the hospital, crowds of people were headed for the train. The injured were carried on the backs of others or they crawled on their own. I got to the station, but the platform, and everything else, was gone. Only the train crossing remained to mark the spot. The train doors were too high up to reach. I couldn't get Saburo inside, and I realized that even if I did, I didn't know where he'd be taken. If he was going to die, I wanted him to be here with us. The roadside was crowded with people who died waiting for the train.

Saburo died a week later, on August 16. My father said, "We still have the others to care for. Can you cremate him by yourself?" I gathered pieces of wood and placed my brother, wrapped in a straw mat, on top of it. Then I lit the wood underneath him with a match. From inside the flames, I heard my brother's joints in his knees and elbows cracking. I can still hear that sound in my head.

As his body burned in the bright red flames, I put my hands together in prayer. Saburo was born on the day of the attack on Pearl Harbor and died the day after the war ended. "Poor thing," I cried.

"You didn't live a single day of peace. You never ate a sweet or got to play. Good-bye, good-bye."

I must have looked terribly sad after that, because when my eight-year-old brother Yoji died the next day, August 17, and then my ten-year-old sister Takiko on August 18, my parents didn't make me watch when they cremated them.

There had been so many of us. We had fought over food, but I loved them all. Now there was only my elder sister, Hisako, and me. Hisako was badly wounded and bedridden. On August 19 she and I were at home alone when I saw a red dragonfly in front of a shed. "Look," I said. "There's a living being flying toward us. It's telling us we'll survive, too!"

My sister asked me to come rub her arms and legs because they were numb. There was glass embedded in her skin, so it felt scratchy as I rubbed it. There were big spots on her body, too. Neighbors had told us about a rumor that the bomb was a new type that emitted harmful gas[1] that made spots. We heard that anyone who got them would die. I felt so sad and helpless.

"Japan is winning the war, right?" Hisako asked. I knew we'd already lost, but I told her we were winning. She wobbled to her feet and said, "Long live the Emperor!" Then she fell down and never got up again.

Hisako was only 14. She had been sent to work in a munitions factory with other girls her age. They had a quasi-military status and had been taught to call out "Long live the Emperor!" if they were about to die. She only did as she'd been told. Later she received a medal, but I threw it away.

I hate the war and the bomb that took my brothers and sisters from me. To tell you the truth, I still feel hatred for America. After the war I ran into a US military police officer. I had picked up an old, broken-down air gun, I swore at the MP, and held the gun up like I was going to shoot him. He put his arms up in fear even though I was just a kid!

My mother died ten years after the bomb. My father, who'd been blinded from the effects of the bomb, died just a year after that. Now I was alone. After the bomb my right ear got infected, and I couldn't hear at all. Years later I had a brain hemorrhage and thought I'd die, but I didn't. I guess my job is to live enough for all my brothers and sisters.

I've forgotten what they looked like. I only remember my elder sister's face.

I started working at the Nagasaki Prefecture Hall when I was seventeen. On my way to work each day, whenever I'd see a pretty girl standing in the train holding onto a strap, I'd wonder whether my sister would've looked like that if she'd lived. I longed to go over to the girl and look at her face, but I never did.

After I retired I rented a large farm and began to grow flowers and vegetables. I've been blessed with children and grandchildren, so I'm mostly happy now. I thought I had gotten over the loss of my brothers and sisters, but even after I got married and had a family of my own, sometimes I'd go up into the mountains just to let myself cry out loud.

I've become a lonely old man. People ask if I'm lonely when I go out to the farm by myself, but it's a good place for me and makes me feel comfortable. Being lonely isn't that bad. It's a kind of strength. I guess that makes me a little different from others.

Staying alive is the most important thing to me. I often tell my story to children, and that's when I think of my brothers and sisters who didn't get the chance to grow up.

I tell the children, "You can't do anything if you die. You can only protect peace if you stay alive."

---

[1]At first no one knew the explosion was caused by an atomic bomb. People thought it was a bomb that emitted gas.

Sanae Ikeda Timeline

1933
Sanae is born on March 24 in city of Nagasaki.

1941
Sanae, aged 8.
December: Japan invades the Malay Peninsula and attacks Pearl Harbor in Hawaii, beginning the Asia Pacific War.

1942
Sanae, aged 9. In June, the Japanese navy suffers heavy losses in the Battle of Midway.

1945
At the age of 12, Sanae begins middle school in April.
August 6: The US drops the atomic bomb on Hiroshima.
August 9: The atomic bomb is dropped on Nagasaki. Suzuko age 6, Sanae's sister, is killed by the bomb.
August 15: Japan accepts the Potsdam Declaration, defining the terms for Japan's surrender.
August 16: Sanae's brother Saburo, age 3, dies of wounds sustained from bomb.
August 17: Sanae's brother Yoji, age 8, dies.
August 18: Sanae's sister Takiko, age 10, dies.
August 19: Sanae's sister Hisako, age 14, dies.

1948
At the age of 15, Sanae drops out of middle school to work and support his bedridden parents.

1951
Sanae is 17 when he is hired by the Nagasaki Prefectural Hall. He begins attending night school.

1981
When Sanae is 48, he begins speaking activities to talk about his experience in the bombing.

2015
At 82, Sanae continues speaking activities and continues planting flowers in town.

2019
Sanae dies at the age of 86.

Dear Mr. Ikeda,

I read your heartbreaking testimony. Thank you for sharing something so personal. I would like to share several verses from my favorite song:

"Even if it's a simple thing, why can't I say it?
If it's an indescribable thing, how can it be communicated?

I forgot the sky that we looked at together,
But I will never forget that we were together.

If you're a flower,
You may not be so different from other flowers,
But, of them all, I chose just one.

There's a song that only I can sing.
There's a song that only you can hear."

"Name of the Flower," by Motoo Fujiwara

I cannot imagine the hardships you must have had to deal with at such a young age, your difficult, painful emotions in having to lose the people most precious to you, one after another before your very eyes. I cannot imagine the depths of your sorrow. And even though I have just read your testimony, I cannot imagine myself in your shoes.

Allow me to introduce myself. My name is Taira, and I was born in 1989 in Chiba Prefecture, surrounded by mountains and fields. I lived together with my father. I dreamed of belonging to an orchestra and started playing the trombone in middle school. When I was seventeen, my father left me behind and disappeared. It wasn't until I was a senior in college that I finally figured out where my father was. He was hospitalized with terminal cancer, and eventually he died.

It was only after my father passed away that I realized how much he truly loved me and how much I loved him, from the bottom of my heart. We didn't have to say a word; we just understood each other. Your testimony reminded me of that, Mr. Ikeda.

The last view of the world seen by your brothers and sisters—Suzuko, Saburo, Yoji, Takiko, and Hisako—and your parents, must have been dreadful. What did they think about? *Who* did they think about? What did they want to do? Thinking about it over and over is very painful for *me*. Right now, at this moment, I struggle to express my mixed-up emotions.

You have struggled with these emotions ever since you were a child. You have suffered alone for such a long time. You have made your way though life with complex feelings of loneliness, pain, hatred, frustration, and more.

I'm curious, what kind of family were you? What was your home life like? What was your favorite thing to have for dinner? What did your home smell like? I have tons of questions to ask you. I believe your parents and siblings in heaven are immensely comforted that you have married, have had children and grandchildren—that you have lived well.

I want to be like you, taking a few steps forward at a time, all while working toward peace in the world.

Best regards,
Taira Ichimura

Taira Ichimura from Chiba, Japan.
Age 26, works for an NPO in Saitama.

Translation by Kwon Bomi from Seoul, South Korea.
Age 22, university student in Tokyo.

Nobuko Yamatani
1925–2012

This Japanese Pioneer in Manchuria
Survived the Chinese Revolution

*"But if my son were still alive and I found him,
I'd just want to be able to tell him how sorry
I was for what I had done."*

*In 1932 the State of Manchuria was established in the northeast
of China as a puppet state of Japan. The Japanese government
launched a national policy to send five million Japanese there
over twenty years as part of the Manchuria Immigration Plan.
In 1944 Nobuko Yamatani became a member of the Manchuria
Pioneers, moving from Fukushima to the Asian continent.
A mere eight months later the Soviets invaded, and the rush
to evacuate began. Even after Japan surrendered to end the
Pacific War, many of the pioneers were left in Manchuria, forced
to survive through the confusion and carnage that followed.
Nobuko married a Chinese man with whom she had a son;
she was forced to give that son up during the chaos.
Long after the war ended she went back to look for her son,
but never found him.*

I was betrothed to a cousin of mine. He had gone over to Manchuria
when he was fifteen. He was the second son of a tenant farmer. His
elder brother would inherit his father's farm, so he had gone over to
Manchuria as a member of the Manchuria Pioneer Youth Volunteers
because there was plenty of land available. The plan was for him to
marry me and settle down there after his army duty was over. A relative of mine who also lived among the Fukushima immigrants in
Manchuria wrote to me, "My husband's gone to war and I'm lonely.
Why don't you come over and keep me company?" I figured since I'd
relocate once I got married anyway, I might as well go now.

I left for Manchuria at the end of 1944. I was nineteen. There
were five houses in the village where I lived, all built the same and
each sheltering two families. When I arrived the war was looking bad
for Japan. All of the men had been drafted, and only women and
children were left.

It was winter and there was no work to do, so I just had fun. I was
told everyone would be busy in May when it was time to plant crops.

They asked me to take care of the children, so I formed a sort of nursery and gathered the children from the village there. When spring came to Manchuria all the flowers bloomed at once: lilies, balloon flowers, Siberian iris, and even peonies. The fields were full of blossoms; it was beautiful.

Then one night, I think it was August 8, 1945, we got a message from the Pioneer headquarters that the Soviets had invaded and we needed to evacuate immediately. Everyone in the tiny village spent the night packing up, and we left the next morning. For every one of us, life was hard from that day forward.

We had been quick to get out and lived close to Jiamusi Station, so we managed to get on a train right away. The bridge just before Mudanjiang, though, had been destroyed. We couldn't go forward, so we went back and transferred to a train for Suihua.

I say train, but it was a roofless freight train to carry pigs and cows. We were packed into it. That August there was a lot of rain, so we were drenched to the skin. There was almost nothing for us to eat or drink, and it was especially hard on the small children. It took more than twenty days to get to a place that could usually be reached in three hours. We finally got to the city of Changchun in September. The children had died on the way, one after the other. Only a few were left by the time we got there, all aged five or older. I felt so sorry for the little ones.

The day after I arrived in Changchun someone invited me to come live and work at a sugar refinery with Chinese owners. I'd heard Japan had lost the war, and I knew I had to do something to stay alive. One of the refinery owners was a widower named Ma Wenjiang. He had a son and was intent on marrying me. Everyone knew, and they teased me about it. The man I was supposed to marry had been taken away by the Soviets, and I didn't expect I'd ever see him again. I married Ma Wenjiang the following February. I was twenty and he was sixteen years older. His son was only ten years younger than me. My husband was a good man, and he took good care of me. If the world had been at peace, I probably would have stayed there for good.

A son was born to us on October 25, 1947, during our second year of marriage. My husband named him Ma Donghai, or "eastern sea." That meant Japan—*me*.

The civil war in China had started to heat up the year before. The Kuomintang, the army of the Chinese Nationalist Party, occupied Changchun, but a few days before Donghai was born the Communist army surrounded the city and destroyed the dam that supplied the city with electricity and water, so we lost both. The gate to the city was blocked, and no food could be brought in. This was the beginning of the starvation tactics by the Communists. Inflation was rampant. In no time at all you could barely buy a single cornmeal cake even with paper money. I would soak a few soybeans, grate them to make soup, add grasses I picked by the side of the road, and flavor it with a little salt. That was all we had to eat for six months. I had diarrhea and suffered from malnutrition; worse yet, I didn't have enough breast milk to feed the baby. I did everything I could to keep him alive.

I finally decided to leave Changchun when Donghai was ten months old. I'd heard that if I managed to get to Shenyang, I could be repatriated to Japan. At first my husband forbade me to go, but after a while he decided there was no other choice. We'd never survive in Changchun without anything to eat.

Donghai and I left the Changchun city gate and entered a place called the *qiazi*, a no-man's land between the entrance to the city and the gate to the Communist-held territory. The date was August 10, 1948. Tied around my neck was a pot with some rice flour and three cornmeal cakes a neighbor had given me. My son was all I had in my arms, and I held on to him tightly.

As soon as we were out of the gate, the Kuomintang army shoved us forward and began shooting. A big man carrying a shoulder pole approached me and snatched the pot off my neck. Now I had no idea what to do. It was August, but the no-man's land was devoid of grass; there was nothing to eat. It was full to overflowing with refugees.

Once we'd left Changchun there was no going back, and it was not a simple matter to get through the gate to the Communist side. They say one hundred thousand people starved to death in the qiazi. Later I heard that the people there cut up and ate the bodies of children who had died. It was a hell of starvation.

We spent the night there, and the next morning a Japanese woman named Soejima, who I'd just met, spoke to me. "I hear they'll let you through the gate if you say you can look after the children of the Communist officials. Leave your baby here and let's go." I knew I couldn't do such a thing. Soejima and I argued about it for a while. Then she told me she knew someone who would take Donghai, and now I had to consider the possibility. Even if I managed to take my son back to Japan, he'd always be known as a Manchurian and considered illegitimate. It didn't seem fair. Maybe it would be better for a Chinese family to take him. I didn't want to, but I finally went along with Soejima.

The next day we left the qiazi area, and I gave Donghai to a family named Li who didn't have children. He had never been held by anyone but me. I'll never forget the resentful look on my son's face when he found himself in the arms of a stranger.

After that I began to look after the child of a Communist official. It just seemed wrong to let an eight-month-old baby of someone I didn't know suckle at my breast. I wanted so badly to go back and get my own baby. I agonized over it, but it just wasn't possible. I tried to forgive myself by swearing that if I ever had another child, I'd dote on him and raise him to be a fine person. Who would ever give up their own child because they wanted to? It's the hardest thing I have ever had to do.

I finally managed to make my way back to Japan eight years after the war was over. In 1953 I arrived by ship at Maizuru Port. It was a miracle. A few years later I married a Japanese man and gave birth to a boy.

When Japan and China finally reestablished diplomatic

relations—when was it?—Japanese children who had been separated from their parents during the chaos after the war were allowed to visit Japan to try and find their families. Whenever photos of these "war-displaced Japanese" appeared in the newspaper I'd scour them for my son. Maybe, I thought, Donghai would be there.

Jisho Yamamoto, the head priest of Chogaku Temple in Nagano, was at the center of efforts to find families of the children left behind in China. He told me children born to one Japanese and one Chinese parent were not labeled as "war-displaced." They hid their Japanese parentage and would never step forward by coming to Japan. Because of the Cultural Revolution no one would admit they had Japanese blood if they could manage to hide it. I gave up after I heard that.

The son from my second marriage grew up and got a job in a bank. He was assigned to Dalian in China. I never could have gone back to China on my own, but my son went with me to Changchun to look for the child I'd left behind. Forty years had passed. I went to the spot where I thought I remembered leaving him, but everything had changed, even the terrain. I didn't know where to start. I looked for the Li family, but never found them.

Back during the war there had been a moat in front of the gate leading to the Communist side. It was completely filled in now and planted with willow trees. It was unrecognizable. Chinese people born after the war probably had no idea what happened there.

At the time I had no choice. But if my son were still alive and I found him, I'd just want to be able to tell him how sorry I was for what I had done. War in any country creates misery and anguish. That's why it is absolutely unacceptable. I've done things that would be unimaginable during times of peace. So much has happened. But I made my own decisions, so I try not to look back.

Nobuko Yamatani Timeline

1925
Nobuko is born on March 7 to a farming family in Fukushima Prefecture.

1931
Nobuko, aged 6. The Manchurian Incident takes place.

1932
Nobuko, aged 7. The Japanese puppet state of Manchuko is established in the northeast part of China. Japanese begin arriving in Manchuko to pioneer it.

1937
Nobuko, aged 12. The Second Sino-Japanese War begins.

1944
At the age of 19, Nobuko sails to Manchuria in December to live in the Fukushima pioneer community.

1945
Nobuko, aged 20.
August 9: Nobuko escapes the community when the Soviet Union invades Manchuria.
August 15: Japan accepts the Potsdam Declaration, defining the terms for Japan's surrender.
September 2: Nobuko arrives in Changchun and learns of Japan's surrender. She begins work in a sugar refinery.

1946
In February, Nobuko marries the Chinese owner of the refinery.

1947
Nobuko is 22 when she gives birth to a baby boy on October 25.

1948
At the age of 23, Nobuko leaves the Changchun city gates in August and enters the qiazi no-man's land. She leaves her 10-month-old son with a Chinese family and becomes a nanny for a Communist official.

1949
Nobuko, aged 24. The People's Republic of China is founded on October 1.

1953
At age 28, Nobuko returns to Japan on a repatriation ship in August. Several years later, she marries a Japanese man and gives birth to a son.

1993
Nobuko, at the age of 68, goes back to Changchun to look (unsucessfully) for the son she left behind. She spends her last years with her son's family in Chiba.

January 27, 2012
Nobuko dies at the age of 86.

Dear Nobuko Yamatani,

In the brightness of the sunlight I can feel that spring is right around the corner. I hope you are doing well. It's nice to meet you. My name is Wu Zhao Hui, and I'm from Tianjin, China. My friends call me Chouyi. Ms. Yamatani, may I call you Nobuko-san?

It is my first time writing a letter like this. I feel like I am in the Studio Ghibli movie *When Marnie Was There*. The thought of writing a letter to an elderly woman when she was my age intrigues me. It feels like passing a tunnel through time.

I came to Japan in September 2007. It was right before I turned nineteen when I left my motherland, about the same age you were when you left yours. I am very surprised at how different our lives have been, at how much the times have changed. While I was reading your story, tears kept streaming down my face. Had you lived in this generation with me, I imagine you might have gotten married to your fiancé and lived a peaceful life. There is so much I want to tell you, but I can't sort out my feelings. My heart is aching, and I can't stop crying.

Reading about war in books, I always thought it was impossible to understand the cruelty of it if you hadn't actually experienced it. As I read your account, though, I felt like I could actually understand it a little bit. I tried to put myself in your place so I could imagine the situation better, but I didn't have the courage to do so. I used to hate Japan because I always looked back to the past. After I came here, though, it was so different from what I had imagined. When you went across the ocean to China for the first time, I wonder how you felt about the land, its language, and its people.

Learning about history from books, it's just a list of names and dates, and we only read the conclusions. The black and white pictures and words portray only facts; books rarely show a human side, people's feelings or their memories. I myself just remembered the outcome

and judged the past by whether something was right or wrong. But my understanding has changed by coming to Japan, visiting Hiroshima and Nagasaki, and reading your memories of that time. When studying about a war fought between two countries for their national interests, we may find out about a past of much darkness and suffering, but looking at things from an individual perspective, we can see that everyone has been a victim. History is shaped by the many people who lived through that time; it cannot simply be judged as either good or bad.

Through my readings, I learned that the relationship between the peoples of China and Japan was much more complicated than it is today. I thought what is commonly known as international marriage today did not occur, but when I read that you had married a Chinese man I felt a sense of happiness. I am glad to hear that your husband took good care of you. It's so wonderful to have a caring husband during difficult times. It's been eight years since I came to Japan, and I have so many Japanese friends. Sometimes I think maybe one day I might marry a Japanese man (hahaha). I hope he will be someone who is caring, just like your husband. I know it sounds very ordinary, but the only happiness I long for is to raise a family.

Nobuko-san, do not blame yourself for leaving your son behind. There is no parent who would *willingly* give their child away. I thought it was very brave of you; you are a mother, and you made the very difficult decision to bear the pain of parting with your son. You chose such a path so that he could survive and be raised without facing discrimination. I believe your son would understand the choice you made. I truly believe that, so please trust me.

I have been writing a lot, but I still feel I have more to say. Participating in a peace seminar and reading your story, I've learned that what is written in history books is doubtless very different from the memories of those who actually lived through that history. People in wars may all have different experiences, but the hope for peace is what they have in common.

Peace was restored, but the cost was high: So many lives lost and so many families torn apart. Although I have limited skills, I promise to use them to contribute toward a world of lasting peace. Nobuko-san, please watch over me.

Sincerely,
Wu Zhao Hui

Wu Zhao Hui from Tianjin, China.
Age 26, office clerk in Tokyo.

Translation by Mihana Higashi Wen from Sydney, Australia.
Age 24, graduate student in Sydney.

Morimichi Tsukahara
1921–201
Starvation and Malaria in New Guinea

*"Don't ever let yourself be deceived
like I was."*

By April 1944 Japan had already lost its air and sea supremacy in the Pacific War to the US and Australian Allies. Morimichi Tsukahara and his comrades knew nothing of this when they landed in New Guinea. The only things waiting for them there were malaria and starvation. Rather than fighting the enemy, some men succumbed to disease, some did unspeakable things to stay alive, and some got lost in the jungle and turned up as cadavers. Of 150,000 Japanese troops sent to the eastern part of New Guinea, as many as 130,000 are thought to have perished.

If I were to sum up my youth, I'd say I was deceived. During the war I was sent to eastern New Guinea (present-day Papua New Guinea). Seven thousand infantrymen in the 115th Regiment from Takasaki were sent there, and only 230 of us came back alive. Almost all of the deaths were from malaria and starvation. Not once did we get rations delivered from Japan. We spent most of our time scavenging for food in the forest. It was a war zone, but there was almost no fighting: just starvation, wandering around, and death. I didn't realize I'd been hoodwinked until after the war was over. I had no idea at the time.

On February 9, 1944 my regiment left Takasaki for Shimonoseki on the night train. We were only told that we were heading south. I had graduated early from Meiji University, gone to officer's school in Toyohashi, and earned the rank of second lieutenant. I was taught that dying in battle was the greatest honor a man could hope for. I knew that the village I was from would throw a big funeral for me. There'd be a sign in the entryway to my family home that said "House of Honor." At the time this was the best gift a son could give his parents. So I wasn't afraid of dying.

From Shimonoseki we boarded sixteen ships and headed south. I was on a ship named *Nanreimaru*. In early March, before we could reach Palau, our fleet was hit by Allied torpedoes. I watched the other ships sink one after another. The soldiers on the sinking ships flailed about in the water, struggling to stay out of the whirlpools the ships made as they went down, but nothing could save them. Only two ships made it to Palau. We stayed there until a new fleet was assembled. When there were eight ships, we left for New Guinea. The same thing happened again. I was on the *Yashumaru*, and it was the only one of eight that made it to our destination. All the rest were sunk. With the first fleet, I was on one of just two ships out of sixteen that made it. The second time only one ship out of eight was left. My chances of survival were so low. It was a miracle that I did.

We arrived at the port of Hollandia in New Guinea and waded ashore. I headed with a group of 150 soldiers to Wewak, in the eastern part of the island where the Japanese army had an airfield. We were ordered to join the troops there.

When we landed we had three days worth of hardtack. I thought we'd find something to eat in the jungle, but I was wrong. We ran out of food quickly and ended up eating anything we could put into our mouths. We ate starch from sago palms, rats, snakes, and maggots. Sloths stunk, and the locals refused to eat them. We buried them in dirt and ate them when the smell wore off. We made salt by boiling down seawater in steel containers. We could live for a week by licking that salt and drinking water.

Soldiers got sick with malaria and paratyphoid. One by one, wracked with fever, they dropped out of formation. Some got delirious and wandered off. There was one military doctor with malaria. He pointed toward the ocean and ordered me "to mark with a dot a spot between that island and that island." He was completely delirious and I felt sorry for him. "OK, I marked it," I said, and he replied, "No, you didn't!" He died not long afterward.

About three days before a man died, flies would start buzzing around him. Next he'd get a bunch of ants in his nose and mouth because he'd lost the strength to brush them away. When I saw that happen to someone, I knew he was a goner.

If a dying man had boots better than yours, you'd say, "I'll take those," and just yank them off his feet and leave him there. It was the same with clothes. Guys you'd been marching with the day before would keel over in droves; there were dead bodies everywhere.

Once we saw a car on the beach and thought we'd met the mobile supply corps. When we peeked inside, though, we saw a mummified body with its hands still on the steering wheel. Looking back, it was horrifying, but by that time, I wasn't scared or even sad. I felt nothing. Death didn't make me feel anything anymore. If I'd felt bad even a little every time I saw a body, I'd have gone mad. That's what a war zone is like.

Some of the starving Japanese troops turned to cannibalism. The army had to make a rule that anyone caught eating human flesh would be shot. One lower-ranking soldier was caught eating his dead superior, and he got shot as punishment. Others who weren't caught in the act still regretted what they'd done and committed suicide.

You hear humans referred to as the highest life form, but in the end, we're just animals—beasts. I was so hungry that I almost became a beast, so I knew how those men felt. When I couldn't stand it any longer, I'd chant my mother's posthumous Buddhist name to get over the temptation. *Junshoin-ryojishozen-daishi, Junshoin-ryojishozen-daishi*. If I kept at it, I'd run out of breath, and for a few moments I'd forget the hunger and fear.

My mother died when I was in the second year of middle school. That day I'd been at an electric appliance shop in front of Ota Station listening to a radio broadcast of the championship game of the annual middle school baseball tournament. That's why I wasn't with my mother when she died. My elder sister told me she'd been calling my name at the end. I was the youngest of five children, and my mother doted on me. After that, whenever I was in a pinch, my mother's face would come to mind. She was the one that kept me from straying off the path of humanity.

In June 1945 we decided that we couldn't fight any longer. We burned our flag to dissolve our regiment—we did this to our flag so that the enemy could never take credit for capturing something we had received from the Emperor. After that we stayed alive so we could serve as "sacrifices." We had been told that—even if we had no hope of winning our fight—if we stayed alive as sacrifices for even a day longer, the enemy would be kept busy having to deal with us, and the Japanese army would have the advantage on another battlefield. So we were not to "die like dogs," wasting our lives by death at the hands of the enemy. If we got to where we could no longer move, we were supposed to stab each other and die.

The war ended on August 15. Allied planes dropped leaflets that said, "The Japanese have surrendered. Stop fighting immediately." Soldiers, however, had been told to ignore enemy propaganda and continue fighting no matter what. Because we'd been ordered to never surrender, even more men died of starvation. There were many Japanese who stole leftover food from the Allies and were shot and killed in the act.

From the day we burned our flag, my men and I were soldiers cut off from the army. I had two lower-ranking soldiers who were in charge of serving me. The three of us stuck together and managed to stay alive. If any of us found food, we'd share it with the other two. We knew that if any one of us failed to share, the other two would do the same when it was their turn. We couldn't survive that way. From this experience I learned the spirit of cooperation. In other words, if I tried to lord it over the other two that I was an officer who'd graduated from military school, I'd die of starvation because the others wouldn't share their food with me.

In October we were captured as POWs and taken to Muschu Island. We were met there by Australian soldiers who shouted, "Cock-a-doodle-doo!" They clapped their hands and laughed, mocking us because we were barefooted, just like chickens.

None of us wrote letters home. There was a rumor that any letters we sent would be stamped with the seal of the prison camp. That's what we were afraid of. We'd been taught that becoming prisoners of war was not an option; that it was more shameful than death.

I finally realized we'd been deceived when the war was over and we got back to Japan. I found out we had been sent to New Guinea after Japan had suffered irretrievable air and sea losses during the Battle of Midway in 1942. Military leaders knew the war was lost, but they kept sending young soldiers to the southern islands.

In spite of all that, I'd miraculously survived to make it home due to the spirit of cooperation that kept my comrades and me alive. After the war, and even after I was running a company in the area I grew up in, I never forgot the lesson of how we'd supported each other on that horrible battlefield. "Cooperation" has remained my motto. I always deal with problems by thinking about the position of the other person. Since I spent my youth being deceived, I make sure I never do anything like that to others.

I'm sure people these days find it difficult to understand the way things were during the war. The lives of my comrades were wasted. They served as sacrifices: starving and wandering around New Guinea until they died. They weren't honorable deaths by any means—they died like dogs.

To the younger generation, who may find my story hard to believe, I'm here to say it really happened. I implore you: don't ever let yourself be deceived like I was.

Morimichi Tsukahara Timeline

1921
Morimichi is born on October 20 in Gunma Prefecture.

1941
Morimichi, aged 20.
December: Japan invades the Malay Peninsula and attacks Pearl Harbor in Hawaii, beginning the Asia Pacific War.

1942
In June the Japanese navy suffers heavy losses in the Battle of Midway.

1944
At the age of 22, Morimichi joins the army after graduating ahead of schedule from Meiji University. He lands in New Guinea in April and begins a march that gets him to Wewak in August.

1945
At age 23, Morimichi dissolves his unit in June and burns its flag; he is left to wander in the jungle.
August 15: Japan accepts the Potsdam Declaration, defining the terms for Japan's surrender.
October 1: Morimichi is sent to POW camp on Muschu Island.

1946
Morimichi is 24 when he is repatriated on the *Hikawamaru* to Kanagawa Prefecture on January 24.

1964
At the age of 42, Morimichi takes post as CEO of Yoshikawa Kogyo, Inc.

1995
Morimichi becomes president, at the age of 73, of the Japan-China Friendship Association of Ota City. Serves until 2006.

March 19, 2011
Morimichi dies at the age of 89.

Dear Mr. Tsukahara,

With sad eyes and a gentle expression, you seem to be looking out at me with a worried face. This spring I became a senior in college, and I am now the same age you were during the war. That is, when you went into battle right after you graduated from college, earlier than students normally do.

A "deceived" youth—that's the way you described your younger days when you signed up (under false pretenses, you feel) for the military. While other ships were attacked and sunk by torpedoes, your ship was miraculously spared. However, what you saw in battle was literally hell. The soldiers starved to death or were infected by malaria and paratyphoid. Your comrades died without even fighting. I know that I cannot fully appreciate what it was like just by reading books or watching films that portray conflicts and massacres. I try to imagine the horrific pictures you saw, but I just can't. The merciless sunlight, the smell of dozens of dead bodies rotting, the warm wind carrying that smell, the sound of the flies and maggots eating the dead bodies, the screams of the injured, it's no wonder you could not let yourself feel anything. When I try to visualize what you must have seen, a dizzying array of macabre images swarm into my mind. How can I possibly understand everything you experienced?

It was only after the war, when you returned to your home country, that you realized you had been deceived. Because you had been lied to, you vowed never to lie to anyone else again. Your wish for young people would be to never ever be deceived like that. For us, I think that's the most important lesson we can take away from your account.

Today we are in "the blossom of youth" while fighting against those who are trying to deceive us. After taking a class at the university, reading a book, and talking with friends, I tried to choose a good spot where we can protest, where we can raise our voices... I did this

because of an incident that happened eight days before you passed away.

March 11, 2011. Until then I was convinced that Japan was a rich, safe, and peaceful country. Because of the nuclear accident that occurred just after the great earthquake, I realized that I did not know anything about the nuclear power plant and that I was involved in its construction without even knowing it. Soon after I began to think about the base in Okinawa, near where I was born and raised for eighteen years.

The thing I fear most is being lied to and not realizing it until it's too late.

We believe our constitution and adherence to basic human rights will protect us from being deceived. These rights are the result of many decades of human effort, and we still have much work ahead. We aim to pass on a better world to future generations. Nevertheless, it's hard to know how or who or what is trying to deceive us. How were you deceived, Mr. Tsukahara? I wish you could have told me that.

I constantly feel uneasy and anxious. Something is going wrong in our society. And here I am, alone, trying instinctively to resist it.

Sincerely,
Jinshiro Motoyama

Jinshiro Motoyama from Okinawa, Japan.
Age 23, university student in Tokyo.

Translation by Derek Matsuda from Chiclayo, Peru.
Age 29, university lecturer in Tokyo.

Yoshio Shinozuka

1923–2014

Volunteered for Unit 731 Youth Corps
at Age Fifteen

*"We were robots who only did as
we were ordered."*

Unit 731 was headquartered in Pingfang, on the outskirts
of Harbin, a city in the northeast of China in what was
once Manchuria. Unit 731 was one of the largest biological
warfare corps in the history of the world. Even before World
War II, biological and chemical weapons were prohibited
by international convention, but despite this, Unit 731 was
developing and producing them. To achieve its goals, the unit
conducted vivisection and other cruel experiments on, and finally
murdered, prisoners of war from China, Russia, and Korea, as
well as anti-Japanese activists. Yoshio Shinozuka knew nothing
about any of this when, encouraged by a friend, he volunteered
for "the devil's unit" in which he spent his entire youth.

Standing on the former site of Unit 731 and verifying what went on there was a difficult thing to do. People were used in experiments, then vivisected and killed. Based on those experiments, horribly lethal gas was produced and used to kill large numbers of Chinese. Those are the facts, and nobody can deny that they are bad.

I still can't believe the things I did. If I had had the sensibilities I have today, I never would have been able to endure any of it. When I was a boy, children started getting militaristic education in elementary school. We believed that anything our commander told us to do was an order from the Emperor, and that we absolutely had to obey. We were accustomed to doing whatever we were told without question.

At the age of fifteen I was studying agriculture in a trade school run by the government. My parents wanted me to be a farmer. I was still in the first year of the school when a friend of mine encouraged me to go with him to sign up for Unit 731. It just so happened that the unit commander was a doctor, so I thought I wouldn't have to fight or kill anyone, and that would make my military service easy. I also knew that if I was in the army, I'd get paid and then I'd be able to go on to university. That was why a lot of guys signed up. Back in those days Japanese were poor, and farmers didn't have a hope of going to university. I had no idea I was signing up for "the devil's unit."

Unit 731 was in Pingfang, on the outskirts of Harbin, a city in the northeast of China. It was part of what was once Manchuria. I worked in Building Ro. The place always had a strong smell of antiseptics, and you could hear sounds coming from it twenty-four hours a day. Bacteria was cultured in the "incubation room," and the sound we heard was the thermostat adjusting the temperature of the room. It wasn't the normal sound of machinery; it was more like the groaning of the devil.

The first time I assisted in a vivisection, I was scared more than anything else. It was terrifying the way that Chinese man glared at us with hatred and contempt. At the time, though, I didn't feel I needed to recoil from him, it was more like I knew I could just ignore him. I think I felt a kind of ethnic superiority. That's what I had learned in school. I didn't think there was anything wrong with it.

Back at the dorm when we were soaking in the bath, we talked about what we'd done during the day. We referred to the people who'd been autopsied alive as "logs." "How many did you cut down?" "Two logs for us today." We didn't act like it was a big deal to take a man's life. We called them logs and didn't think of them as human beings.

After a few years, when I figured out what was going on, I wanted to get out. I still thought what I was doing was right, but it got harder to put up with. The more I learned about bacteria, the scarier it got. It wouldn't have been so bad if I didn't know anything, but I figured it out, and I felt like I was going mad. I started to have delusions that I was close to dying. In fact, many of my comrades died after being infected by bacteria. As I watched them die, I was sure the same thing lay ahead for me. None of us knew when it would be our turn.

No matter what the situation is, no one ever wants to give up their own life. It's human instinct to try to save yourself. On top of that, I realized that in the unit, the men at the top never did the work that was really dangerous. They made the men under them do it. Then they took credit for the results. Once I figured that out, it all seemed so ridiculous, and I tried even harder to save my own life. The tough part was that once you were in the unit, you were stuck there until the end. There was no escape.

War involves a basic contempt for life. If that weren't true, there never would have been a Unit 731. When you're dealing with a person one on one, then you can respect their life, but once the people in charge tell you you're doing it for the Emperor, everything changes. There was a line in the *Imperial Rescript to Soldiers and Sailors* that said, "Your life is worth less than the feathers on a bean goose." We'd had that drilled into our heads, so we believed it. I didn't even know what a bean goose was.

There was a child of a Chinese prisoner on the grounds. Probably living in Building 7 on the second floor. When the weather was good, the kid would take walks outside with its mother—in the Ro courtyard. The child was just learning to walk. I saw them from up on the roof, so I couldn't make out the shape of the child's face or anything.

When Japan surrendered, the unit destroyed Building Ro and many other facilities. All of the documents were burned in the incinerator, even after August 15 when the surrender was final. They killed all of the prisoners that were left and threw their bones into the Songhua River. That's what I heard. It was all done to get rid of the evidence.

I didn't think they'd murder that child. Then I heard later from a guy on the transport squad that they'd done the same thing to the kid as they'd done to the others. That guy was haunted by dreams about that child. Almost everyone who was in Unit 731 had dreams like that.

After Japan surrendered, I and some other soldiers spent time in the Chinese People's Liberation Army. As an inmate at the Fushun War Criminals Management Center, I learned the truth about Japan, and it opened my eyes. I was finally able to look objectively at what I had done. The most important part of my time there was living in a section called Rokusho with the generals and other Manchurian dignitaries. Without that experience, I never would have found out what the top brass in Japan was thinking when they went to war. If I'd never been held in the Fushun War Criminals Management Center, I would not have known the crimes I had committed; I would never have been able to reflect on what I had done. I regret my crimes from the bottom of my heart. Without my time in prison I might not feel the need to apologize to the victims or even feel guilty for what I did.

While in the People's Liberation Army and at the Fushun War Criminals Management Center, I always had the words *shi shi qiu shi* in my head. It is a Chinese saying that means "facts are the source of everything." In other words, if you look at the facts, you'll naturally understand what is right, or conclusions come out of facts. Unfortunately, facts are multifaceted and look different depending on who is seeing them. Still, only one side can be right. I always take this stance when looking at and thinking about things.

I was in Unit 731 from the age of fifteen until I was twenty—my entire youth. Unit 731 destroyed my ability to think for myself. It took away my power to make decisions. We were robots who only did as we were ordered. We could not distinguish good from evil. I don't think wars are possible without it taking people into dark places like that.

War is ruthless and indiscriminate, so I believe we should not go to war or have an army. The fact of the matter is that Article 9[1] of the Japanese Constitution has kept this country at peace ever since the end of World War II. That's why we have to protect and follow it. What need do we have to destroy peace?

---

[1]Article 9—Aspiring sincerely to an international peace based on justice and order, the Japanese people forever renounce war as a sovereign right of the nation and the threat or use of force as means of settling international disputes. In order to accomplish the aim of the preceding paragraph, land, sea, and air forces, as well as other war potential, will never be maintained. The right of belligerency of the state will not be recognized.

Yoshio Shinozuka Timeline

1923
Yoshio is born on November 1 in Chiba Prefecture.

1931
Yoshio, aged 7. The Manchurian Incident takes place.

1932
Yoshio, aged 8. The Japanese puppet state of Manchuko (Manchuria) is established in the northeast part of China.

1937
Yoshio, aged 13. The Second Sino-Japanese War begins.

1939
At the age of 15, Yoshio applies to join the youth division of Unit 731 in February. He is assigned to Unit 731 headquarters in Manchuria in May.

1945
Yoshio, aged 21. On August 15, Japan accepts the Potsdam Declaration, defining the terms for Japan's surrender.

1946
At age 22, Yoshio serves in Chinese People's Liberation Army.

1949
Yoshio, aged 25. The People's Republic of China is founded on October 1.

1952
Aged 28, Yoshio surrenders himself as a former member of Unit 731 and is sent to Fushun War Criminals Management Center.

1956
Yoshio is 32 when he is exempted from prosecution during the war criminals trial in July, released, and sent back to Japan. He gets a job with the Chiba government and marries.

1984
At age 60, Yoshio retires from his job and begins war-survivor witness activities. He makes many trips to China to apologize and pray for the souls of the dead victims.

1997
At 73, Yoshio erects a stone monument at Myofukuji, a temple near his home, to apologize for Japanese actions and promise to maintain friendly ties with China.

April 20, 2014
Yoshio dies at the age of 90.

Dear Yoshio Shinozuka,

My name is Daikichi Kato. I am an ordinary college student. You may think that I am fortunate to be able to go to school. Because everyone has the right to study these days, I live in a better environment than you did during the war.

If I were in the same position as you were during the war, would I have been able to refuse a senior officer's order or object to the experiments? Although it was experiments on live human beings, I might have done it if it meant I would be able to go to school, if it meant escaping poverty and having a more stable life. Especially if it was during a war, when looking ahead to the future seemed impossible. In such a situation, would I be able to stop killing and listen to my conscience? I probably wouldn't have been able to. I would have made myself believe that the person I was going to kill was something other than a human, or I would have believed, as you were taught, that I was superior to Chinese people and killed with hatred and contempt. Either one would have convinced me to continue the experiments. Based on the education you received in that era, how could you have done otherwise?

The Chinese person in front of me who I was going to kill may have had a family, probably chatted with friends, may have had a lover, or some incredible talent, all of which would have made him the same as me. But if you erase this mindset and all sensitivity, what you are left with is war.

You were understandably worried, knowing that you were being made to choose between the dignity of life or your own life. Although you must have wanted to enjoy your carefree teenage days, you were working every day in an institution called Unit 731, in which your job was to conduct human experiments. The majority of the people there must have kept quiet about what they were doing and continued to do their duty. Or perhaps they had already been deprived of their ability to think. The more they committed these cruelties, the more desensitized they became.

There are probably some people who never told a soul about what they did during the war just so they could save face. You could have done so as well, but you chose not to. You have faced what you did during the war. You went to China many times to apologize, and you admitted to everything. You have not lost your humanity.

I really do respect you. Why? Because I don't think I could ever have been so brave. I'm afraid I would have pretended that nothing had happened, convinced myself that I had done the right thing, and gone on to live my post-war life.

"How many logs did you cut?"

I would have been one of those people who boasted about it even now. That is the crucial difference between you and me.

I think I can understand how much courage it takes to tell those haunting stories over and over again. It must be a heavy burden to carry. I would like to praise your determination. You have done this for a long time; I appreciate it and hope to learn by your example.

I believe that there are no heroes in war. No matter how well the story is told, it will always be a tragic event. People experience horrendous losses and people die.

I am lucky, I know, not to have experienced war directly. I am strongly against it and hope for peace. But honestly, I sometimes feel empty because I haven't been tested. Because I have not had to endure an era of war, I fear I could not rise to the challenge, and I don't trust that I have what it takes to bring about peace in the world.

Even now you must hate the war so much. At a time in your life when you were supposed to be going to dances and stealing kisses, war forced you to end human lives without knowing why. I will tell your story to as many people as will listen. And if they will not listen, I will shout it from the rooftops. In order to prevent the ravages of war from devastating another generation, I will continue to tell your story.

With respect and appreciation from the bottom of my heart,
Daikichi Kato

Daikichi Kato from Tokyo, Japan.
Age 24, university student in Tokyo.

Translation by Naoki Ueda born in Singapore.
Age 19, university student in Tokyo.

Taeko Shimabukuro
1928–
The War in Henoko, Okinawa

*"We survived the war—why provoke another one
by building a new base?"*

The Battle of Okinawa was a bloodbath that resulted in a huge number of casualties, including civilians. The people living in the middle to southern part of the main island of Okinawa were caught up in the fighting. In comparison, Okinawans like Taeko Shimabukuro, who lived in Henoko in the north, suffered less from the US landing and bombings. From Henoko though, so-called defense and guerrilla forces were sent further north, and this resulted in even more victims. Taeko's father was drafted into the Defense Force and never returned to his family. More than two hundred thousand died in the fighting. Among them was one quarter of the Okinawan population. The war finally ended, but Okinawa was forced to accept US military bases. Even today the citizens of Henoko are faced with plans for a new base. In short, the war has never really ended for the people of Okinawa.

I was born and raised in Henoko. I've never lived anywhere else. As a child I spent more time helping out my family than going to school. I was sent to the mountains to gather firewood. I was supposed to put it on my head and bring it home, but it was too heavy and made me cry sometimes. We never had money, but we always had enough food.

The sea off Henoko was beautiful and clean. It was full of good things. Crabs, shrimp, shellfish—everything. We ate them in broth. We planted potatoes and other vegetables in the fields, and the mountains were covered with firewood, which we traded for soy sauce, somen noodles, and cooking oil. That was how we made a decent living. The old lady next door called the mountains the Green Leaf Bank. I thought that was so clever.

Camp Schwab, a US base, now occupies the place where our vegetable gardens and rice paddies once thrived. And they're talking about building another base here in Henoko. Military bases are for wars. We survived the war—why provoke another one by building a new base?

I entered a girls' school when I was sixteen or seventeen; this allowed me to work and pursue studies. Henoko wasn't bombed much at first. But during the October 10 air raids,[1] I was mobilized, along with other girls, to build a pier in Henoko. A squadron of three planes flew slowly over our heads. We had no idea what they were up to. We thought they were on our side. The soldier with us told us they were Japanese planes, so we all threw up our arms and yelled *Banzai! Banzai!* But it turned out they were the enemy.

In April 1945 bombs started falling on Henoko. Banyan Park was a spot where everyone liked to relax, and there were several houses with thatched roofs nearby. When the park was bombed, all those houses caught fire. There was no time to get water out of a well, so we formed a bucket brigade to carry seawater, but we couldn't put the fires out.

When it was too dangerous to stay in town, we Henoko residents went up into the mountains and dug out an air raid shelter and built a simple house. We hid there for a while.

The Japanese troops were starving, just like the rest of us. When the soldiers heard about a house with food in it, they'd show up and aim their guns at the people living there. The Japanese soldiers thought we'd stolen their rice. We'd say, "Look around for yourself. We've only got our own rice and potatoes," and the soldiers would leave, but if someone's mother or grandmother picked some green soybeans and left them by the river, the soldiers would steal them. Then the mothers would go get them back. There were lots of soldiers that didn't care about civilians. As long as they survived, it didn't matter what happened to anyone else.

My father was forty-one. Shortly before the Americans landed on Okinawa, he was drafted into the Defense Force[2] and sent to Mt. Yaedake in Yanbaru (in the northern part of the main island).

About the same time I saw a truck full of boys aged maybe fourteen or fifteen. They were all carrying bamboo spears. I think they were in the Gokyotai Corps.[2] They passed through Henoko on their way north, but I think they were attacked on the way. There were so many boys and men from around here who were killed in the Defense Force and the Gokyotai Corps.

The war ended, but my father didn't come home. I refused to believe he was dead. I was sure he was still alive somewhere. I'd heard that some soldiers were captured as prisoners of war and taken as far away as Hawaii. My father's sister lived in Hawaii, so it made sense to me that he was living there with her.

We learned of his death three years after the war ended. The battle in the north of Okinawa ended on April 20, and we knew he was still alive at that time. We'd heard he told his friends he was going to return a gun he had been given to safeguard, and then he would head home. They didn't know what happened after that, but we think he was killed in a rice field in a place called Haneji. In Okinawa there are people called *yuta* who tell fortunes. We asked a yuta what happened to my father, and that's what we were told. It turns out there is a cenotaph built in memory of the war dead in a village upstream from Haneji.

I think the last time I saw my father was in March. It was shortly before the Americans landed. The Defense Force arrived in Henoko to say good-bye, and we had a big send-off party and there was drinking.

Maybe my father was already missing us. The next day he came to the house, and then went right back to his troop. But I remember I came out of the house, and there was my father looking at me. That was the last time. I was still young and had nothing to say. I never thought he'd really die. He was short and didn't talk much; he was a kind father.

After the war I married a man from Henoko. So many young people had died in the war that parents were eager to get their children married off quickly. My husband came from a wealthy home, and he was a gentle man. I heard that his brother had died in the war as a kamikaze pilot—on May 25, 1945. When I heard that, I remembered something.

It was just about that time that I saw a plane emblazoned with the Rising Sun. It circled Henoko Bay and then flew off. I remember thinking it was strange because the fighting had moved south by then. I decided that the plane I saw must have been my husband's brother coming to say good-bye. After that he probably flew to the sea off Itoman and sacrificed his life. He wasn't even married yet.

After the war Henoko was full of bars. I ran a bar for a while, too, during the Vietnam War. A lot of the customers were US soldiers. I didn't understand anything they said, and I didn't know how to serve whiskey either, but the young women working with me helped.

I'm sure the US soldiers going off to war were certain they'd never make it home—not the way they were drinking and spending their money. They were drowning their sorrows in liquor. They'd get nasty and violent, and then they'd cry. I felt sorry for them. War is bad. Any war. America and the US army killed my father, so I can't forgive them for that, but decades have passed. There's nothing to be gained from holding a grudge, so I don't bear them any ill will—but I haven't forgotten the war.

My father and my brother-in-law died in a rice paddy and in the ocean. I wonder if they ever reached Nirvana. How could either of them be resting in peace after dying that way?

How could anyone who still remembers the war be in favor of a new base? That's why I go out with the other old people to demonstrate against it. We all go to our doctor's appointments and then to physical therapy. We do our housework, and then we go to sit-ins on Henoko Beach.

All it takes is one airplane flying over us to drown out our conversation. It's a terrible racket. If they build a base here, they'll have to reclaim land from the beautiful ocean to do it. I've never seen a dugong,[3] but I'm sure the old fishermen have. I'd rather jump in the sea than let them build that base, but there are more of us old people than can fit in a boat. The only thing left for us to do is hold a sit-in at the beach to protest.

There are people who lost their parents and brothers and sisters in the war who want the base because they'll make money off of it. I ran a bar, so I understand where they're coming from. But some things are more important than money. There's a saying in Okinawa that life is our treasure, the dearest thing we have. Anything you do is fun as long as you're healthy. You can't trade money for life, can you? That's something you only understand when you get older.

Young people don't know war. Are they going to have hard lives, or happy ones? We may not be around ten years from now, but we're worried about what will happen to Henoko. That's what we old folks talk about while we sit on the beach.

---

[1] October 10 air raids—On October 10, 1944 the US carried out large-scale bombing of Okinawa. Ninety percent of homes in Naha, the capital, were destroyed, and about six hundred people were killed.

[2] Defense Force, Gokyotai Corps—Mainly in Okinawa, boys from the age of seventeen to men of forty-five were drafted to supplement Japanese forces on the ground. The men were called the Defense Force. The Gokyotai were young boys under the draft age mobilized into undercover and guerilla troops. They were caught up in the fighting and many of them died.

[3] Dugong—A dugong is an endangered sea animal found as far north as Okinawa; it is a relative of the manatee. Many organizations are joining the movement to protect the dugong feeding areas and are protesting the US base construction work going on in Henoko.

Taeko Shimabukuro Timeline

1928
Taeko is born on August 15 in Henoko, on the main island of Okinawa.

1941
Taeko, aged 13.
December: Japan invades the Malay Peninsula and attacks Pearl Harbor in Hawaii, beginning the Asia Pacific War.

1944
At 16, Taeko witnesses the October 10 air raid of Okinawa.

1945
April 1: US forces land on the main island of Okinawa. Henoko suffers an air raid, and Taeko's father is killed in fighting in the northern part of the island.
June 22: The Japanese army is defeated in the Battle of Okinawa.
Taeko, aged 17.
August 15: Japan accepts the Potsdam Declaration, defining the terms for Japan's surrender.

1951
Taeko, aged 23. The Treaty of San Francisco is signed in September. Okinawa is put under the administration of the US.

1972
Taeko, aged 43. On May 15, Okinawa reverts back to Japan.

1997
Taeko is 69 when Henoko becomes a candidate to replace the US Futenma Base in Okinawa. She participates in anti-base activities as a member of the Protect Life Group and the Dugong Group.

2014
Taeko, aged 85. A politician publicly opposed to the Henoko base construction is elected governor of Okinawa.

Dear Taeko-san,

I'm thankful that you survived the harsh war. And I'm so happy that you are still alive. I couldn't stop crying when I read your story.

You cannot get back what you lost in the war, and for that my heart aches. Although you were almost the same age as me back then, you lost your loved ones and your town was destroyed. I am the second child of five in my family and am a daddy's girl. My eyes were full of tears while reading the part where you say, "I refused to believe he was dead" for three years after the war. I can't imagine what you must have felt when you found out your father had been killed in action. I don't think I could have borne up under the dreadful situations you experienced. I'm sure I would have cried and cried, day after day.

I actually went to Henoko, Okinawa, for the first time last month. I saw where you were born and raised. I went to Camp Schwab to do a sit-in, and I saw a lot of older men and women. You and I might have passed by each other. Just the thought of it puts a lump in my throat.

It's been seventy years since the war ended. But it hasn't ended for you in Okinawa because Ospreys are still flying overhead, and military vehicles are running around everywhere! My heart skipped a beat, to be honest; it must be so frightening. I didn't know the real circumstances that Okinawa is facing until I went there. People in Okinawa have made their feelings known regarding the base many times. However, the current Japanese government has ignored your pleas, and they are forcing you to live with the base. I feel scared and anxious because the government has trampled on democracy, and it feels like any minute now we may really go to war again.

You said, "We may not be around ten years from now, but we're worried about what will happen to Henoko." The people of Okinawa have experienced, and survived, the horrors of war, and they say "No more wars." I cannot believe that both the US and Japanese govern-

ments are forcing another US base on Okinawa.

I saw a lot of elderly people in front of the gate at Camp Schwab, and I'm sure many of them were alive during the war. They have had hard lives, but they are using the remaining years of their lives to protest the military base. Their eyes seemed so kind, yet sad at the same time. But I also saw in them their strength and determination. I know they will never give up.

I met many students and young people who are against the US military base. It is important to pass on the memories of elderly people about the war for the sake of future generations. Remembering the war experiences and keeping up the campaign against the military base to prevent wars in the future are vital missions for all of us.

We should never again make others go through the same nightmare you did, Taeko. And we should never let anyone destroy the beautiful sea in Henoko for the sake of war. As you said in your story, "There's a saying in Okinawa that life is our treasure." We must demonstrate the importance of this with every action that we take.

When I save up the money and my school is on break, I want to go to Henoko again.

I hope I can meet you then.
Motomi Okada

Motomi Okada from Shizuoka, Japan.
Age 18, high-school student in Shizuoka.

Translation by Mao Kamata from Miyagi, Japan.
Age 21, university student in Gunma.

Hiroko Iwami
1934–

After the War, Suffering from the Atomic Bomb Dropped on Hiroshima Continued

"The hardest time for me was when I was eighteen and nineteen years old. I don't know how many times I wished I'd been burned to death in the bomb."

At 8:15 on the morning of August 6, 1945, when it seemed that Japan was very near surrender, the US military dropped an atomic bomb on Hiroshima. It was the first time ever such a bomb had been used. Hiroko Iwami, aged ten, suffered terrible burns and lost her eyesight in the explosion. Despite her injuries, she managed to escape from the destroyed city. She survived, and the war ended. Japanese society began its recovery and people's lives became more comfortable. For Iwami and other atomic bomb victims, though, the end of the war was just the beginning of their trials.

The bomb was dropped the summer I was a fifth grader at the Hirose Elementary School, but my family was moving that day. We were part of the "building demolition" scheme[1] and got evicted, so my parents, grandmother, aunt, elder sister, younger brother, and I moved to our new home in the Hiratsuka neighborhood right before the explosion. I was planning to continue going to school in the Hirose area, so I only survived the bomb because I'd spent August 6th with my family. I would have been dead if I'd gone to school. That part of town was close to the epicenter and was completely demolished, or so I heard.

I was thrilled when we arrived at our new house. I ran upstairs once and then came back down. When I went outside again, I heard a dull humming sound and could see some B-29 planes flying overhead, leaving behind contrails in the clear, blue sky. I counted one, two, three planes, and then I heard a bang and everything went white. The wind from the bomb blew me back into the house.

I think I passed out. My father pulled me out of the rubble of our possessions that had been piled up in the house's entrance. He must have felt relieved that we were all safe. He ordered us to escape to Mt. Hiji, about a mile away. Then he ran to help our new next-door neighbors.

My father didn't notice that my skin was peeling off and hanging from my body and that my face was black. I heard later that my hair was standing straight up. I had terrible burns from my neck to my back as well as on my face. And my eyes—I couldn't see anything.

After that, I had no idea how we managed to get away. People seemed to be everywhere, running back and forth in confusion. The bridge to Mt. Hiji might have been burned down. I heard someone yell out, "We can't cross the bridge!"

Because I couldn't see, I didn't know what was happening. I was separated from my mother, sister, and brother. My grandmother and aunt pulled me along. I was wandering around in the dark. My feet were bare as we walked over glass and rubble. The bottom of my feet hurt, but my brain was so foggy I couldn't really feel anything.

We ended up at a military facility, the East Parade Grounds, which was close to Hiroshima Station. People around me kept encouraging me to pull myself together and someone gave me a tomato to eat.

I'm sure many victims of the bomb were there. Throughout the night I could hear people moaning and groaning. Voices were saying things like, "He's already dead" and "If they die, we'll have to carry them out of here."

The upper half of my body was so badly burned that no one thought I'd make it. To tell you the truth, the pain was unbearable.

The next day we crossed the mountain and arrived at Yaga Elementary School. My father showed up, having heard that I might be there. I found out afterwards that he looked me over and said I wasn't his daughter, that's how altered my appearance was. I vaguely recall hearing my father's voice and wondering why he couldn't find me. Finally he called out my name again, "Hiroko!" I guess I answered and that's how he knew it was really me.

After that we moved to the Shinonome Armory, and that's where we were when the war ended. Then we were taken in at the Hachihonmatsu Public Hall. It took about a month for my eyes to recover. But then the flesh on my shoulders scarred into a lump, and I got weeping keloids on my face that wouldn't heal.

I finally stopped going out at all. I couldn't go to school because my scars were so bad. I didn't have any friends. Once I put on a hat big enough to hide my face and went to the movies by myself. The person sitting behind me told me the hat was ruining his view and I needed to take it off. So I couldn't go to the movies either. I lost my entire youth.

After a few years, you stopped seeing people like me with keloids. According to doctors, most of them died. The reason I survived despite my burns might have been because I didn't go into the city after the bombing.

Since my education was ended partway through elementary school, I got a job at a printing plant where my father worked so I could learn to read. I was sure no one would ever marry me, but someone did come along. My husband had escaped from Manchuria after the war ended. He told me he'd seen horrors. Groups of people would be in hiding from the invading Soviet troops, and a crying child could give them all away. My husband saw parents strangling their own children to death to keep them quiet.

My husband was kind to me and said, "The people in Hiroshima are strange. Everyone was affected by the bomb, but they discriminated against you and you couldn't find a husband—that wasn't fair."

I wasn't sure about having children because I had been exposed to so much radiation, but I was blessed with two healthy daughters. When they were born, an employee from the US Atomic Bomb Casualty Commission (ABCC)[2] came and brought me flowers. They said they wanted to inspect my babies. How did they know? After I was injured, ABCC had come to pick me up in a Jeep. They made me take off all my clothes and inspected every nook and cranny. I hated it.

ABCC would tell you what the results of your tests were, but they wouldn't treat you...probably because we were the ones who lost the war. Even today we have to do what America tells us to.

During my recovery from the radiation, I vomited blood many times, and I felt lethargic. The worst part was the scars from the burns. My left ear was stuck flat against my head. I wished so many times that I could have surgery to repair it. My mother was old-fashioned and always told me that I couldn't harm my body further by cutting it.

Much later, when my elder daughter was in high school, she encouraged me, saying, "Mom, if you want to get surgery, why don't you?" Thanks to her, I was finally able to make the decision to do it.

My daughters never asked me about the bomb, but they must have been concerned about me. After all, I never went to any activities at their schools.

Surgeons took skin from my stomach and grafted it onto my face. They couldn't do it all at once, so I had several surgeries. When the new skin on my face didn't take, it turned into keloids and I had to redo the surgery. It was hard on me and painful, but when it was done and my face looked good again, I felt like I'd been reborn. I began taking every opportunity to go out. I took trips and enjoyed going to the hair salon.

After that, when I told people I was a *hibakusha*, someone who had suffered from the radiation of the bomb, people said they'd had no idea. When I was a child, I'd been carefree and daring—I went back to being like that.

The hardest time for me was when I was eighteen and nineteen years old. I don't know how many times I wished I'd been burned to death in the bomb. The city was recovering, but I felt like I remained a victim.

Recently, though, I've been to elementary school reunions and heard about the atomic bomb experiences of others. There were so many who died without leaving a bone behind. When I heard those stories I realized that I was luckier than some others. Still, it's only recently that I can go out and talk to people.

We can't have wars—none at all. It won't be long before the

atomic bomb is only a story that gets passed down. But we must never forget how so many people suffered from it and died, and how many continued to suffer after the war was over.

---

[1] Building demolition scheme—Since buildings were built so close together, fires caused by air raids spread from house to house easily. To keep the damage to a minimum, buildings were destroyed to create firebreaks.

[2] US Atomic Bomb Casualty Commission (ABCC)—Offices were set up in Hiroshima and Nagasaki to study the effects of radiation from the atomic bombs. The Japanese government also participated in the research. Victims of the bombs were highly critical of the program because they were examined but not offered any medical treatment.

Hiroko Iwami Timeline

1934
Hiroko is born on September 20 in city of Hiroshima.

1941
Hiroko, aged 6.
December: Japan invades the Malay Peninsula and attacks Pearl Harbor in Hawaii, beginning the Asia Pacific War.

1942
Hiroko, aged 7. In June, the Japanese navy suffers heavy losses in the Battle of Midway.

1945
At age 10, Hiroko suffers severe burns on the left side of her body after the US drops an atomic bomb on Hiroshima on August 6.
August 9: An atomic bomb is dropped on Nagasaki.
August 15: Japan accepts the Potsdam Declaration, defining the terms for Japan's surrender. Hiroko does not return to school, but learns to read while working in a printing factory with her father.

1965
At the age of 30, Hiroko marries and subsequently has two daughters. She undergoes several surgeries to transplant skin on her face.

2007
At 72, Hiroko sees a film in August based on the victims of the atomic bomb from the school she went to, and participates for the first time in the annual commemorative service for those who died in the bombing.

Dear Hiroko-san,

Hello, my name is Kaede Nagashima and I am from Fukushima. I am nineteen years old—the age when you were the most distressed about what the bomb had done to you.

I know I am lucky; I was able to attend the schools that I wanted to and study the subjects that I wanted to from junior high school through university. And it is all thanks to people like you. You struggled desperately to survive the war and pass the baton of life on to the next generation. You also worked mightily to rebuild Japan's broken economy. Thank you, Hiroko-san, for fighting to stay alive. Because you survived the atomic bomb, you are a piece of living history that links us to the past. You are very kind and generous to share your difficult story.

It breaks my heart to think how horrible it must have been, and how much pain you must have endured, when the atomic bomb was dropped on Hiroshima by the B-29 called the Enola Gay. Even though you couldn't see and had no shoes on, you had to flee through masses of people, over broken glass and splintered wood. I remember playing with a friend when I was a child. She blindfolded me and then led me around by the hand. It was scary, but it doesn't compare with your experience. I'm sure that I would not have been able to get through the circumstances as courageously as you did. You are so strong, Hiroko-san. I hate the war for making you think: "I wish I'd been burned to death in the bomb" and "I lost my entire youth." Along with the importance of life, you showed me just how fortunate I am to be alive at this moment.

I believe that people have the ability to learn from the past. However, they don't seem to appreciate that happiness comes from a life that is simple and peaceful. People don't think about war, or history, or the lessons that you and the other A-bomb survivors have to teach us. We need someone to remind us how good our lives really are

and to wake us up to what happiness really is. This is what your A-bomb experience did for me. I need you, Hiroko-san; please stay alive.

I am from Fukushima City, and I was exposed to radiation emitted by the Fukushima Daiichi Nuclear Power Plant disaster. On March 11, 2011, I was fifteen years old. I had no idea about radiation exposure at that time, so I went out right after the accident when the radiation level was 20 microsieverts per hour. I have neither physical pain nor obvious symptoms like you had, but I, too, am worried about the effects of radiation exposure on my body and on my baby if I get pregnant. So I know how you must have felt! I am terribly anxious when I think about the risks of pregnancy and of getting cancer, but I know I can't spend all my time worrying about what might be. Hiroko-san, you have also had these anxieties, and you overcame them. Your life reminds me that I should live my life to the fullest, with positivity and optimism.

With gratitude,
Kaede Nagashima

Kaede Nagashima from Fukushima, Japan.
Age 19, university student in Saitama.

Translation by Kaho Ichimura from Iwate, Japan.
Age 25, graduate student in Tokyo.

Lee Hak Rae
1925–

Went from Guarding POWs on the Thai-Burma Railway to Death Row Prisoner

"I want to…restore the honor of my friends who died so needlessly."

Korea and Taiwan were colonies of Japan, and many people from those two countries were mobilized for Japan's war efforts. One of them, Lee Hak Rae, served as a guard in a POW camp in the South Pacific. After the war he was tried as a Class BC war criminal and sentenced to death. He witnessed the execution of his comrades, but managed to avoid it himself. He was sent to several prisons, including Changi in Singapore and Sugamo in Tokyo, spending a total of eleven years as a prisoner. When he was finally released, he began living in Japanese society for the first time. He and other former prisoners started a taxi company in an effort to make a living. Lee has been active in making appeals to the Japanese government to solve the issue of former Korean Class BC war criminals.

In 1925 I was born into a family of Boseong farmers in what is now Jeollanam-do, South Korea. Korea was annexed to Japan in 1910, so fifteen years had already passed.

In elementary school we were forbidden to use Hangul, the Korean language. At our morning assembly we bowed in the direction of the Emperor in Japan and recited the Oath of Imperial Subjects.

In 1940 Koreans were ordered to change to Japanese family names. Koreans named Lee and Kim chose Japanese names that retained a hint of the original. Most people wanted to keep the names that had been passed down to them through countless generations, but they didn't want to be singled out for bad treatment, so most followed the order. My name, Lee Hak Rae, became Hiromura Kakurai. "Hak Rae" and "Kakurai" were written with the same characters, but Kakurai was pronounced in the Japanese way.

I was sixteen when the Pacific War began. The next spring one of my friends heard from a city official that men were being hired to guard Japanese POWs in the South Pacific. He told me the contract was for two years and the pay was fifty yen a month. He urged me to go with him to apply. A few days later I appeared before the city official for an interview. At first he rudely ordered me to leave. The job description was for men aged twenty and older. I was only seventeen and so not qualified, but then he and a police officer told me it didn't matter and that I should go; I couldn't object.

I thought it would be safer than being sent to the mines in Hokkaido or to the battlefields as a soldier. I took the test and passed. When I left home my grandmother was crying. "I'll never see your face again," she said.

In June 1942 three thousand and several hundred guards for the Japanese army were rounded up in Korea. We were inducted into the Temporary Military Education Corps (Noguchi Force), and subjected to two months of strict training. We had to memorize the *Imperial Rescript to Soldiers and Sailors*, the *Senjinkun Military Code*, and the *Oath for Army Civilian Employees*. Our trainers would use any excuse to beat us: small voice, poor posture, badly cleaned weapons. They hit us so many times. What I hated most was slapping each other's faces. We were forced to do it in pairs, facing each other and trying to see who could slap the hardest. It was a stupid thing they made us do to please the superior officers.

Our training ended in August, and we were shipped out to the South Pacific. My destination was a POW camp upstream on the River Kwai in western Thailand. My orders—along with those of five other Korean guards—were to move five hundred Australian, British, and Dutch POWs to Hintok, which was even farther inland. The Thai-Burma Railway was being built to take Japanese troops to invade Imphal in India. The railway became famous in the movie *The Bridge on the River Kwai*. My job was to supervise the POWs who were building it.

Hintok was deep in the jungle where humans rarely went. It was dark even during the day. We cleared out the area, built a dormitory, and began work on the railroad. The environment was terrible, and the prisoners were emaciated and starving. They were overworked as well as suffering from malaria, dysentary, and cholera. There was no medication or medical facilities to treat them. More than one hundred died.

At first the only supervisors were we Korean guards, so I might have seemed like a commander, but I had no real authority at all. We had been ordered to provide labor for the Japanese railway corps. If I was told that three hundred men were needed on a certain day, I had to make sure I had that many. If I couldn't get enough, I had to negotiate with the leaders of the prisoners to get workers who were not too sick to work.

Some of the POWs failed to follow the rules. When discovered, we would chew them out and give them a slap or two. That sort of behavior, though, went against the Geneva Convention and was considered abuse. Nobody told me that. We Korean guards had never even heard of the Geneva Convention—we were trained by being slapped around, so it seemed the natural thing to do.

After the war four Australian POWs charged me with war crimes, and I was sent to Changi Prison in Singapore. I was given almost nothing to eat and was beaten and kicked. I felt bad about the POWs who had died, but I was only following orders and didn't think I was to blame. A captain in the Noguchi Forces finally claimed responsibility for what happened in Hintok, and my charges were dropped. I was let go, but on my way home I was recaptured when my ship docked in Hong Kong. I was sent back to Changi. This time I was charged by nine Australian POWs and tried by an Allied military tribunal. On March 20, 1947 I was charged as a Class BC war criminal[1] and sentenced to death.

When the judge proclaimed "Death by hanging!" I had no idea what had happened. I was handcuffed and brought back to my senses by the cold metal on my wrists. I was led off to P Hall where death row prisoners were held until execution.

Death sentences were usually carried out about three months after sentencing, so I knew how long I had left. There was a courtyard in the concrete hall surrounded by about twenty cells.

When I arrived, there were about fifteen other prisoners, one of whom was Korean. The general atmosphere was not one of sadness and depression; the Japanese prisoners were proud to be able to die for their country. For us Koreans, though, it was different because we wouldn't be sacrificing our lives for our own country.

I thought long and hard about what I would be dying for, and for whom. There were many Koreans who had died fighting the Japanese colonization policy. I had been forced to mobilize, but when it came down to it, I had cooperated with the Japanese war and was being executed for abusing POWs. I wondered how much my parents and siblings were suffering for my sins. I was guilty of betraying my own people.

On the day before an execution an Indian captain would arrive with the notice. We prisoners would be in the courtyard playing *go*, but when that captain showed up, we all went quiet. The names of the prisoners to be executed were read aloud.

That night those men were taken to another place and given their last meal. The next morning, as they were taken to the gallows— which was right next door to us—the doomed men would call out, "Departing now!" and we could hear feet marching. Soon after we heard the Japanese yell out, "Long live the Emperor!" Koreans screamed, "To independence!" Then we heard a banging noise and knew that the execution was over.

The day before the other Korean, Rim Young Joon, was executed, I asked to accompany him at his last meal because he was the only prisoner scheduled to die. His Japanese name was Hayashi. He didn't eat anything or say a word. He seemed to just be waiting quietly for the time to pass. The next morning, as we were saying good-bye, he took my hand and said, "Hiromura, get your sentence commuted. I want you to live so you can tell people that Hayashi was not such a bad guy."

I couldn't say anything, because I was going to die, too. All I could do was squeeze his hand back.

I spent eight months on death row wondering when my turn would come. In the end my sentence was reduced to twenty years. It might have been because I had been tried, released, and then tried again.

I was moved to Sugamo Prison[2] in Tokyo. While I was there, the San Francisco Peace Treaty was signed, declaring that Koreans were no longer Japanese. I thought that was a good reason to get released, but nobody listened to me. I was finally released in October 1956 and went out into Japanese society for the first time. I didn't know anything about it.

I thought about going home, but back in Korea war criminals were considered Japanese collaborators.[3]

In Japan I had two friends whose situation was the same as mine. They committed suicide from hopelessness due to isolation and the difficulty of making a living. One stepped into the path of an oncoming train, and the other hung himself on the grounds of a temple. Another friend never recovered from the shock of being declared a war criminal. He became mentally ill and spent forty years in a Japanese hospital. He died at the age of seventy-eight. He had no idea where he was. When he heard fireworks going off in the summer, he thought it was bombing. He had no contact with his family on the Korean peninsula and didn't know whether they were dead or alive.

We war criminals had limited job opportunities. We learned how to drive in Sugamo Prison, so we all had driver's licenses. We thought we could all work in a taxi company. With the generosity of a doctor named Tomofumi Imai, we started our own company with ten cars.

We didn't want to lose anymore of those of us who were left. We worked as hard as we could for the sake of those who had died and were determined to make a go of it. In this way I worked for twenty-five years with my friends. There are only four of us left alive.

In 1991 I went to Australia and met the former POWs who had accused me of crimes. I hated them for a while. But when I thought about it, I realized they had lost many of their comrades while building the Thai-Burma Railway. It was no wonder they had lashed out at their Korean guard. I apologized to Colonel Dunlop, who had been the leader of the prisoners. I told him I, too, had been mistreated in Changi Prison, and he and I were reconciled. Colonel Dunlop died two years later. He was a great man. He put his life on the line to protect the other prisoners every time he had to negotiate with me for laborers.

We Koreans were sent to war for the Japanese. Some of us died after the war as Japanese citizens, some of us endured long years locked up in prison. The San Francisco Peace Treaty, however, took away the Japanese citizenship of Koreans and Taiwanese, which meant that we could not receive post-war compensation or much other support. The Japanese treated us as their own when it was convenient, and when it no longer suited their purposes, they told us they had no responsibility for us. How unfair was that?

I like the Japanese. But I want the Japanese government to apologize and compensate Class BC war criminals. So far I've sent requests to twenty-nine prime ministers over sixty years, but they have never responded. The courts recognized that we had been victimized, but dismissed our suit and told government officials that they "expected appropriate legal measures to be taken."[4]

I want the Japanese government to admit their illegitimate actions, earnestly accept the opinion of the courts, and take measures promptly to comfort the souls of the departed and restore the honor of my friends who died so needlessly.

Once again I want to make an appeal to the common sense and moral fiber of Japanese citizens.

[1] Class BC war criminals—In the trials held by the Allies after the Asia Pacific War, Class A criminals were those who committed "crimes against peace" by conducting wars of aggression. Class BC war criminals were those who were guilty of "inhumane treatment such as abuse of prisoners of war." Five thousand seven hundred soldiers were tried as Class BC war criminals. About one thousand, including 23 of 148 accused Koreans and 21 of 173 accused Taiwanese, were executed.

[2] Sugamo Prison—A Tokyo prison built for war criminals in November 1945. On December 23, 1948, Hideki Tojo and six other Class A war criminals were executed there.

[3] Status of war criminals in South Korea—In 2006 ex-soldiers tried as Class BC war criminals were officially recognized as having been forced to mobilize rather than willingly cooperate with the Japanese, and their honor was restored.

[4] Trial and legal framework—The Japanese government was sued for apology and compensation. In 1999 the Supreme Court recognized the damage caused by the government, but dismissed the suit. In 2008 a proposal for a bill to provide special benefits to specific detainees in Allied trials that would compensate Class BC war criminals was presented to the Japanese Diet, but the Diet was dissolved without ever considering it. Lee Hak Rae continued to call for consideration of the bill each time a new Diet was opened, but in 2014, when it became clear that the matter would not be resolved in Japan, Lee made a petition to the constitutional court in South Korea.

Lee Hak Rae Timeline

1925
Lee is born on February 9 in present-day Jeollanam-do, South Korea.

1940
At the age of 15, Lee changes his name to a Japanese name, Kakurai Hiromura, under orders from Japan to give up his Korean name.

1942
At 17, Lee is trained in June in Pusan to be a guard at a Japanese POW camp. In August, he begins work as a guard in a POW camp in Thailand.

1945
Lee, aged 20.
August 15: Japan accepts the Potsdam Declaration, defining the terms for Japan's surrender. Korea is freed from Japanese rule.

1947
At 22, Lee is put on trial in Singapore on March 20, given a death sentence as a Class BC war criminal, and sent to Chiangi Prison to await execution. (The sentence is eventually commuted to twenty years in prison.)

1950
Lee, aged 25. The Korean War begins in June.

1951
At 26, Lee is transferred to the Sugamo Prison in Tokyo in August.

1952
At the age of 27, Lee loses Japanese citizenship in accordance with The Treaty of San Francisco in April.

1956
At 31, Lee is released from prison in October. He and other former Class BC war criminals start up a taxi company.

1991
Lee, age 66, meets with former POWs he guarded in Australia.

2008
Lee, aged 83. A proposal for compensation for Class BC war criminals is presented to the Japanese Diet, but the Diet is dissolved without ever considering it.

Dear Mr. Lee,

It's a pleasure to meet you. I am Hiroyuki Ohmura, one of the young Japanese who has no memories of the war. I read your story, and I learned about a Japan that I never knew.

After I read your account, I thought about how the war had taken away not only human life, but also human dignity. You said that some Japanese people took pride in dying for their country, but you would not be dying for anyone or anything because Koreans had been forced to become Japanese. You also worried about what would happen to your family after you died as a war criminal. Rim Young Joon's last words to you were "Get your sentence commuted. I want you to live so you can tell people that [I] was not such a bad guy." These words made me think hard about the significance of death without honor. Later on you suffered from the indignity of not knowing how to make a living or what you should live for.

Part of the military training you underwent as a POW guard was surely meant to have you question your sense of morality and values. Why were human beings treated with such disregard? We need to hear more about the rage, hatred, and grief of the war years.

As students we learn only the superficial details of Japanese colonialism: the policy of forcing Koreans to change their names, for example. It was not until I read your story that I understood the profound implications of colonialism and its policies. It's cruel to deny basic freedoms such as using the names people were born with and the languages they grew up speaking. The fact that you were denied your identity so completely saddens me. People love their own countries, and the language of those countries is a fundamental part of that affection. I am ashamed and bitter that this was done in my name.

I've never experienced war, but my grandparents and great-grandparents did. They lived through the war and through the post-war

years. Since my life is an extension of that past, I need to live in the present and build the future I want to see, while acknowledging and accepting the past. Your words tell me how important this is.

Thank you for your testimony, Mr. Lee. You are "not such a bad guy."

Gratefully,
Hiroyuki

Hiroyuki Ohmura from Niigata, Japan.
Age 22, university student in Miyagi.

Translation by Yun Hyun O from Osaka, Japan.
Age 25, university student in Tokyo.

Fusako Iwase

1923–2018

Evacuated from Tokyo to Nagano
Leading a Group of Schoolgirls

*"Life is the most important thing we have.
That's what I learned from the children
I evacuated with."*

As the war situation deteriorated, children from big cities were evacuated to rural areas to keep them safe in case of air raids. Fusako Iwase was only twenty-one and a brand-new teacher when she accompanied a group of Tokyo schoolchildren to a country town in Nagano Prefecture. She did her best to be a mother to the homesick girls. Then came the surrender. The US commander General MacArthur and his GHQ gave orders for a new kind of education, and Fusako started the next phase of her life full of unease about what lay ahead.

I always wanted to be a teacher, and I got my wish in 1942, the spring I turned eighteen. Japan had bombed Pearl Harbor a few months before, in December 1941. I still remember the day clearly. My usually calm father was reading the newspaper and his face darkened as he spat out his words.

"Going to war with America! We'll never win. Those fools!"

Later, when I left the house, I looked back at our laundry hanging from poles in the yard and swinging in the breeze. The sky was so blue. I remember wondering if a war could really break out when the world seemed so peaceful.

After that society moved steadily in the direction of working for the war effort. We were told, "luxury is the enemy." Women were encouraged to scold anyone who got their hair permed. At the national people's school,[1] where I was working, the male teachers were sent off to war one after the other. At first our mornings began with rousing music like Beethoven's "Turkish March," and then one day it became "If I Go Away to the Sea," a military song about dying for the sake of the Emperor. Whenever I heard it, all I could think about was bloody, dead soldiers in the ocean and corpses being rained on in the mountains. I still hate that song.

In August 1944 the war was getting closer to home, and I was sent to Tokura Onsen in Nagano Prefecture to evacuate with the third-grade girls from my school. I was in charge of about twenty students. They all wore backpacks and acted like they were going off on a field trip, but the parents who saw them off at the station were full of anxiety. The mothers hung on to my arms, giving me instructions like "she catches cold easily, so keep an eye on her" and "be sure to wake her up so she doesn't wet her bed." As I looked at them, I realized uneasily that I was going to have to be a mother to all these little girls.

My charges, of course, were only happy for a few days before they got homesick and wanted to go home. Even out in the country, food became scarce and the children were hungry. They ate the adzuki beans their pillows were filled with. Each evening we all gathered in a circle for dinner. When suiton was on the menu I got one extra flour-and-water dumpling in my soup because I was an adult. I could feel the children's eyes on me, but I couldn't just give one girl an extra dumpling, so I quickly drank my food down. I couldn't taste anything.

Separation from their parents was the hardest thing for the girls to endure. When we took walks along the banks of the Chikuma River, we'd come to a field dyed bright yellow with evening primrose that was as tall as the girls were. They'd run into the field to play, but if we heard the whistle of a steam locomotive heading to Tokyo, all of their little heads would turn in the direction of the sound, and they would cry for their mothers. I held them close as they sobbed—I wanted to cry along with them. After all, I was only twenty-one myself.

Occasionally the parents came to visit and the children eagerly looked forward to those occasions. There was one little girl named Keiko. Once, her visiting mother left to go home while Keiko was still at school. Heartbroken, the child ran to the station to look for her mother, but the train had already gone. Keiko walked back along the tracks, crying the whole way. When I heard about this later, much later, I also found out that since she wasn't supposed to cry in front of the others, she carefully wiped her eyes before going back to the inn where we were living. They were forced to endure so much.

I'll never forget the summer of 1945. In the middle of the night there was a loud sound and the ground rumbled. The air raid sirens went off. American B-29 bombers had come all the way into the Nagano mountains. I woke up the girls sleeping on the second floor of the inn, but I wasn't sure what to do next.

I gathered them on the first floor and called out their names to make sure they were all present. There was a large room next to the entrance where I had them lie down with their heads together and their legs spread out in a circle like the spokes of a bicycle tire. I covered them with futons and then lay down on top of them. "Don't you dare get up! Don't even lift your head!" I yelled. I have never scolded anyone like that before or since. All I could think about was not letting them jump up.

Fortunately no bombs were dropped, but I thought my heart would burst from terror. I never thought about myself, I could only think about protecting these little girls their parents had entrusted to me.

I still see them from time to time, and they talk about that night.

"I can still feel the weight of the futons on my shoulders."

"Sensei, you were so scary!"

"You were heavy."

It's funny now, but that was the weight of life.

We were told that Japan was winning, but I knew that if B-29s were flying over Nagano we had to be losing. The children and I lined up in front of the inn to hear the "Jewel Voice" radio broadcast of the Emperor announcing Japan's surrender on August 15, 1945—the speech where he talked about "enduring the unendurable and suffering what is insufferable."

Japan had really lost the war. I felt as heavy as if I'd drunk lead. How was I going to gather these children and tell them the truth? I was afraid they'd break into tears.

When I finally made the announcement, they were all quiet for a few seconds. Then one girl, a tomboy nicknamed Sugi-chan shouted out, "We're going home! I'm going to see my mother and father!" That was the end of the solemnity. The girls were all delighted and flew about the room like butterflies. I sank down on the floor in relief as I realized our lives were no longer in danger and that the children and I had all survived.

The girls taught me then and there that staying alive was the most important thing in the world. Everything I am today started from the day Japan surrendered.

That didn't mean I felt good all of a sudden. I had taught the children that in Japan, nothing and nobody was more precious than the Emperor. Once I had even taken my class to Niju-bashi, the double bridge across the moat surrounding the Imperial Palace. We went and paid our respects to the Emperor.

I could claim that I didn't know any better, but I was afraid that I could be charged with cooperating with the war effort. It was a difficult time to be a teacher. I didn't know what would happen to the country. The teachers collected all of the children's textbooks and blacked out all words praising the war, although I didn't know what that was supposed to accomplish. I was afraid we might end up having to obey everything the US told us to do.

A year later I got married and left my job when I got pregnant.

I lost my confidence, but the new Basic Act on Education and the Japanese Constitution gave me hope. My eyes were wide with amazement as I read about them in the newspaper. I was really happy then. What finally helped me recover from the war was Article 9[2] of the Constitution, which talks about abandoning war. I knew then that I could make a new life for myself.

After I raised three children, I wanted to study this new democracy that we got after the war. I had many reasons, but the main one was that I had learned from the war that not knowing was a sin.

I learned about Fusae Ichikawa.[3] I was born in the year of the wild boar, so I tend to rush headlong into things. Whenever something sounds wrong to me, I rush in to take care of it. That's why I've been involved in peace activism and doing things to make my area a better place to live. I started a group, Izumi-no-kai, in my neighborhood to teach children about the war. I organized showings of movies about life in Japan during the war, such as *Barefoot Gen* and *The Glass Rabbit*, and invited parents to bring their children.

Despite all that, we've entered an era where society no longer seems to understand that life is much too important to ever go to war again.

Life is the most important thing we have. That's what I learned from the children I evacuated with. I'm going to keep telling people that for as long as I live.

---

[1] National people's schools—Schools set up in April 1941 to replace the conventional school system. There were six years of elementary school and two years of secondary school, for a total of eight years of compulsory education. The goal of the school was to educate children to become citizens who would give their lives for the Emperor and for the country. The focus was on strengthening the body and mind through courses categorized as National Citizen Studies and Physical Training.

[2] Article 9—Aspiring sincerely to an international peace based on justice and order, the Japanese people forever renounce war as a sovereign right of the nation and the threat or use of force as means of settling international disputes. In order to accomplish the aim of the preceding paragraph, land, sea, and air forces, as well as other war potential, will never be maintained. The right of belligerency of the state will not be recognized.

[3] Fusae Ichikawa (1893–1981)—A leader of the women's movement in Japan from before World War II, she fought for women's suffrage and played a role in getting women's rights included in the post-war constitution. She was elected to the Japanese Diet in 1953 and served five terms, including one that she began in 1980 when she was 87.

Fusako Iwase Timeline

1923
Fusako is born on June 28 in Chiba Prefecture; her family moves to Tokyo.

1941
Fusako, aged 18.
December: Japan invades the Malay Peninsula and attacks Pearl Harbor in Hawaii, beginning the Asia Pacific War.

1942
April: Fusako starts work as an elementary school teacher.
June: The Japanese navy suffers heavy losses in the Battle of Midway.

1944
At the age of 21, Fusako evacuates to Nagano with schoolchildren in August.

1945
Fusako, aged 22. On August 15, Japan accepts the Potsdam Declaration, defining the terms for Japan's surrender.

1946
Fusako marries and retires from teaching.

1947
Fusako, aged 23. On March 3, Japan's Constitution goes into effect. After raising three children, Fusako studies democracy and is inspired by Fusae Ichikawa.

1981
At the age of 58, Fusako starts a peace study group in her neighborhood and begins many years of related activities.

February 9, 2018
Fusako dies at the age of 94.

Dear Fusako-san,

I am in my mid-20s and have been working as a schoolteacher for four years. When I was a student I often had the feeling that teachers, *sensei*, were adults living in a different world from me; I didn't like them very much. Indeed, I often subjected them to my confused feelings so particular to adolescents. At that time I never imagined that such a childish girl would become a schoolteacher. Even today, when I run into my old teachers, I realize how wonderful they were. I cannot thank them enough.

After I started to earn my own living and began being treated as an adult, my grandmother told me stories of what it was like to be a *hiba-kusha*, an atomic-bomb survivor, born in Nagasaki. Her tragic account brought the war home to me. I came to see the truth in what my grandmother often said: "Eating as much as one pleases is happiness" and "Taking a family trip is wonderful." Little by little, I realized what she meant. She had lived during a time when what I take for granted would have been luxuries beyond her wildest dreams. We have no idea what it was like to live through the war. I've come to understand that it is our responsibility to learn.

Thank you, Fusako-san; reading your essay gave me the opportunity to see the war through your eyes. I found you were around my age when you were a teacher, and what you experienced brought up a heartrending question for me. Over and over again I wondered, "If I had been in Fusako-san's place, what would I have done?" I cannot begin to picture what my life would be like if Japan were engaged in a war. Your loneliness, pain, fear, and anger at that time are beyond my imagination. I understand that saying I feel empathy with you would be sheer arrogance. I really don't know anything.

It may sound a bit strange, but I am pleased to find that some things have not changed: adults can still learn things from children.

When the war finally ended, I'm not surprised that there were few adults shouting, "I survived!" or "I can see my family!" with the fullness of joy your students did. I am sure that in the militaristic society of Japan back then, only children were able to honestly express their feelings about missing their families.

Now I spend my days with my students at a junior and senior high school. Because I am a teacher, sometimes I praise or scold them, at other times I devote myself to just spending time with them. I am looking forward to seeing my students in the future when they are grown and, hopefully, succeeding out in the world. Even now, though, these boys and girls teach me lots of things. I see this in the unexpected questions they ask me and when they argue passionately with each other. Children can do freely what we grownups cannot. I am sure you felt this way when you were a teacher.

I know I am still learning as a sensei, but I have lived longer than my students, and I want to pass on the knowledge that I've inherited from the past to future generations. I will tell them about you, Fusako-san—such a great sensei, who always put her pupils' safety above her own.

Sincerely,
Yukino

Yukino Takei from Kanagawa, Japan.
Age 26, teacher.

Translation by Makiko Endo from Shizuoka, Japan.
Age 28, teacher in Kanagawa.

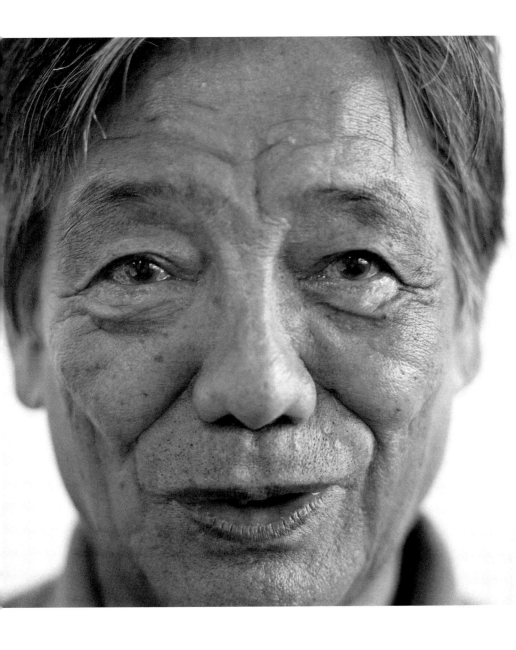

Koyu Kinjo
1928–2010

Mobilized in the Tekketsu Kinnotai Corps
During the Battle of Okinawa

"If anyone ever tries to send you to war, don't give your country a second thought. Run!"

Two hundred thousand souls were lost during the Battle of Okinawa, one in four of the people living in the prefecture. The war was in its closing days, and boys in middle school and older were drafted into student troops called Tekketsu Kinnotai ("Iron and Blood Corps Working for the Emperor"), a student signal corps. In March 1945 Koyu Kinjo graduated from Okinawa No.1 Middle School and was inducted into the Tekketsu Kinnotai the same day. His first job was to write his will. As the fighting got worse though, the boys were allowed to leave the corps and go home. Kinjo left and escaped with his mother and younger brother, heading south and away from the fighting in Shuri. The three of them survived, but other boys who stayed with the corps were caught up in the US invasion. Most of them died.

My earliest memories are of living in Shuri, the ancient capital of Okinawa. I learned the Okinawan language from my grandmother and grandfather. I didn't speak Japanese at all until I started school. At first I couldn't understand a thing the teacher said, so it was tough, but I didn't let it get me down. I was so full of energy that I was nick-named Bochira, which means stubborn and mischievous—something like "rascal."

On October 10, 1944, while I was only fifteen and still in my fourth year of middle school, the air raids began in Okinawa. We saw dozens of US fighter planes heading toward us, and then hundreds. School let out and we were told to go straight home.

Instead of doing as I was told, I went up a hill where I could see the whole town in flames. I just stayed up there and watched. I remember that I wasn't scared, but I knew in my heart that Japan had lost the war. When Saipan fell to the Allies, I read the headlines: "No planes, lost opportunities." The military insisted that this was a lie, but anyone who read the newspaper regularly could see what was happening. Japan had no chance of winning the war.

On March 24, 1945, I was three days away from graduation. By then the US was conducting air raids in preparation for landing, and I had evacuated with my family to a bomb shelter. Ikehara, a classmate, came to report that a student corps named Tekketsu Kinnotai was going to be formed after graduation and that joining up would not be optional. Nowadays parents would probably object, but things were different back then.

Our graduation ceremony was held in the evening as night began to fall. Air raids always stopped as the sun was setting, so we waited for the lull. Yasushi Shinohara was the military officer assigned to our school. He spoke at our graduation, turning the occasion into an induction ceremony: "Starting today, all of you are members of the Tekketsu Kinnotai." We didn't get to go home, so our teachers collected our diplomas and we never saw them again.

Next we were ordered to write our wills. I wrote that I would "die in service to the Emperor." I was patriotic to the militaristic country that Japan had become and wanted to write something smart. I put my will and a lock of my hair into an envelope and handed it to my teacher.

I didn't die, but many of my friends did, so they really did draw up their last will and testaments that day. Many of the boys in Tekketsu Kinnotai were killed. Not all died in battle, though. Some were behind the front lines, but got hit by bombs. My good friend Ikehara died in the Battle of Okinawa, but it was after he had left the corps.

I was a private second class, so I had a star on my uniform, but my job was to dig holes. My corps had a shelter in a place called Tamaudon, the tomb of Ryukyu monarchs. Every day we commuted to the army headquarters in Shuri to dig a shelter for the top brass. We also did maintenance work. I knew the area well, so once it was my job to lead repairmen to the place where communication lines had been cut. As I got ready to set out from headquarters, the lieutenant colonel gave me a hand grenade.

"This is not to throw at the enemy," he said. "If you're ever captured, use it to kill yourself." Fortunately I managed to make it home without having to use that grenade.

I was in Tekketsu Kinnotai for a month. At the beginning of May Commander Shinohara had an announcement. "If you've got family and can get to them, you're free to leave." Later, when I thought about it, it didn't make sense to send soldiers home in the middle of a war. I guessed that the corps had run out of food and needed to cut their numbers.

Nineteen of us left. My friends told me that I could be tried for desertion in a military tribunal. Others called me a weakling, but I was starving. People nowadays have no idea. Food was all I thought about. If I saw someone moving his mouth, I was certain he was eating something.

I felt wretched about deciding to leave because of food. But that move saved my life. The ones who stayed got caught in the US offensive and many of them never made it home. The names of my friends who died in the war are engraved in a memorial on the site where our school dorm once stood. I still think about them. I remember their faces, their voices, their personalities, and even the grades they earned in school.

When I got home I learned that my father had been drafted. My mother was alone with my five-year-old brother. I carried my brother on my back, and the three of us headed south to escape the Americans.

By the end of May the Japanese army had disintegrated. Soldiers, scattered and destitute, were left to scavenge for food. That was all that was left of the defeated forces. On June 17, I think it was, two or three days before I became a POW, I ran into a few Japanese soldiers walking along the Mabuni shore. The ranking officer had a light machine gun.

"I don't have any bullets, so I don't know what I'm doing with this," he said, and tossed the gun into some weeds. I couldn't believe it. He was talking about a weapon provided by the Emperor. I was surprised, and I knew for sure that the country was finished.

As we escaped south we saw lots of dead bodies. I'll never forget the corpse of a mother who had been hit by a bomb. Her baby died still clinging to her. The child had probably been alive until a few hours before. It was so heartbreaking I could hardly bear to look.

Let me tell you who I blame for what happened: the leaders of Japan during those years. It's like it says in Sun Tzu's *Art of War*— what happens if you "know neither yourself nor your enemy." It was a stupid war.

We just kept going, doing our best to escape. Finally, on June 19, we were captured in a place called Yamashiro, close to Kiyan, at the southernmost tip of Okinawa. I think it was about ten at night. We were in a group of about twenty men and women hiding in a pigsty. The US soldiers showed up, and we were cornered.

The Americans had been dropping flyers that said, "Come out and surrender. We won't kill you." They were written in Japanese. We had heard rumors that the Americans were not killing people indiscriminately, so we began to walk slowly out of the pigsty.

The Americans shot off a flare that was too bright to look at. When it was gone, we saw a row of US soldiers standing before us with rifles drawn. One of the soldiers spoke Japanese.

"You have been saved. Sleep in this hole tonight," he said. Before our eyes was a hole made by a bomb from a battleship. It was about ten tatami mats in size. As soon as I realized we weren't going to be killed, the first thought that came to mind was, "I'll be able to sleep tonight." The whole time we'd been on the run, I hadn't had a single peaceful night of rest. It started raining after midnight, and it felt like we were sleeping under a water tap. We got soaked. But nobody woke up. We didn't have to worry about being killed. We weren't going to be bombed. Rain was nothing compared to that! I slept like a log.

The next day we were marched into Itoman, where we were transferred by truck to the POW camp at Futenma. A week after we arrived the war ended. There were so many Japanese POWs, but the Americans didn't make us work. Bulldozers did the work of a thousand men, so they didn't need people to help. It was a surprise, but I finally realized what sort of country we had been up against. No wonder Japan lost.

I was only sixteen at the time, and a "rascal," right? I got bored doing nothing, so I left my mother and brother and escaped the camp. I wasn't lonely or afraid of anything, and I never got emotional. I always knew I'd make it somehow.

Later I worked in a US camp. My father never came back from the war, and I knew that Japan had been treated cruelly, but I was more afraid of Japanese soldiers than Americans. Japanese soldiers slapped me, but US GIs never raised a hand to me.

When I was a university student, I passed a test to go to the US and study. I went to a school in the state of Maine. Later, when I got a job, most of my work involved transactions with companies in other countries. I made friends and acquaintances all over the world. I don't hate anyone now.

Americans will often say they fought a humanitarian war, and this is what I tell them, "Listen here. You killed a lot of civilians along with the soldiers." Even if they disagree, I refuse to give in. "I was one of those civilians. It's true that the Germans and Japanese were wrong, but the Americans didn't come out of it smelling like roses." I saw it right in front of my eyes. Many, many civilians were murdered.

Nowadays you'll never catch me saying anything like I would "die in service to the Emperor." I'm not a pacifist, but I would do anything to protect my children and grandchildren from having to go to war. There is not a single benefit to be had from dying in battle. People remember dead soldiers for a while, but not long. Only their mothers remember and mourn them.

That's why I tell young people, "If anyone ever tries to send you to war, don't give your country a second thought. Run!"

Koyu Kinjo Timeline

1928
Koyu is born on December 15 on the main island of Okinawa.

1941
Koyu, aged 12.
December: Japan invades the Malay Peninsula and attacks Pearl Harbor in Hawaii, beginning the Asia Pacific War.

1944
At the age of 15, Koyu witnesses the October 10 air raid of Okinawa in Naha on his way home from school.

1945
Koyu, aged 16.
March 27: Koyu graduates from middle school and joins the Tekketsu Kinnotai Corps.
April 1: The US forces land on the main island of Okinawa.
May: Koyu quits the Tekketsu Kinnotai and escapes with his mother and younger brother to the south of the island.
June 19: Koyu is captured as a POW by the US forces.
June 22: The Japanese army is defeated in the Battle of Okinawa.
August 15: Japan accepts the Potsdam Declaration, defining the terms for Japan's surrender.

1951
Koyu, aged 22. The Treaty of San Francisco is signed in September. Okinawa is put under the administration of the US.

1952
At 23, Koyu studies as an exchange student at a university in Maine, USA, while enrolled at University of the Ryukyus. After graduation he is employed by a trade company, for which he also served as an interpreter, living overseas as well as in Japan.

1972
Koyu, aged 43. On May 15, Okinawa reverts back to Japan.

August 12, 2010
Koyu dies at the age of 81.

Dear Mr. Kinjo,

The scent of spring is wafting through the air, and buds are about to bloom. It is nearing the season you joined Tekketsu Kinnotai, right after you finished middle school many years ago. I wonder how the weather was back then. I assume it was already hot in Okinawa at the end of March. How did you feel when you were drafted into the unit? As you said, you followed militarism at that age; you might have been thrilled, energized by the hot Okinawan air. However, you were just a kid. Leaving a last will and testament with a lock of your hair in an envelope, expecting to die on the war front, is not what a fifteen-year-old boy is meant to do. Now Japan is so peaceful; it is hard to imagine what happened back then.

I would like to tell you about myself. My father is Korean and my mother is Japanese. My nationality is Korean, and I am a fourth-generation Korean citizen living in Japan, what is called Zainichi. My great-grandparents on my father's side moved to Japan when Korea was a Japanese territory.

After the Meiji era, Japan, having been introduced to imperialism by the US and European countries, proceeded to colonize Taiwan, Korea, and northeast China. As a result of this so-called loyalty to the Emperor, I exist as a Japanese-born Korean, a living reminder of a war that took place between the two countries. During the war you were involved in, no one complained about the countless deaths of friends and other young people. Colonizing and killing were considered reasonable ways to win the war, out of loyalty to the Emperor. That is horrifying.

You said you were a rascal. Reading your story, I can picture you doing everything possible to escape the American POW camp where you were imprisoned. My image of war is no longer one of utter hopelessness. I believe it when you say, "If anyone ever tries to send you to

war, run!" It shows what a rascal you were, and it explains how you managed to survive. Your character gave you a strong will to live. That is why your words have the weight of truth. Although your story was one of tragedy, I found hope in your character. Thank you for telling your story.

With best regards,
Lee Young Ho

Lee Yeong Ho from Kanagawa, Japan.
Age 27, part-time employee.

Translation by Ai Kawashima from Gunma, Japan.
Age 21, university student in Gunma.

Masaji Shinagawa

1924–2013

Member of a Frontline Combat Unit in China

"If human beings start wars, then human beings can stop them."

Masaji Shinagawa was drafted into the army and shipped to China, where he was sent into the thick of the fighting and barely managed to escape with his life. As a student, Shinagawa had studied philosophy and long pondered the meaning of life. For him, the most difficult part of being a soldier was the loss of identity. After the war he was sent to a prisoner of war camp. The following year he was finally repatriated. On the ship home, he got a glimpse of a draft of the new Japanese Constitution. Back in Japan he became one of the business leaders who took Japan into its period of rapid growth, but he never stopped thinking about why wars happen.

I received my draft notice in November 1944. I was twenty. As I was a student of Sanko High School (the present-day Kyoto University), I should have started my military career as a commissioned officer, but I ended up going off to war at the low rank of private second class.

But there was a reason for that. When the military came to our school to check on our preparedness, a good friend of mine purposely made a mistake when reading out a passage from the *Imperial Rescript to Soldiers and Sailors*, a book all of us had received. Instead of saying that the army existed for the purpose of serving the Emperor, my friend said that the Emperor existed for the sake of the army.

One of the officers caught the "mistake" and almost killed him. The entire school suffered. There were calls for everyone from the principal on down to submit their resignations, and the survival of the school itself was on shaky ground for a while.

I was the student leader at the time, so I sent out a petition that said I would join the army as a private and agree to go to the front lines if the school was allowed to continue. At the time I was sure I would die in the war whether I was a private or an officer, and I didn't really care which it was. I heard that my friend who made the original fuss committed suicide while I was away at war, but I never learned the truth of what happened to him.

At the time we students were making lists of books we wanted to read before we died. One guy wanted to read *The Tale of Genji*, so when he skipped classes to do so, teachers looked the other way. It was a very liberal atmosphere.

There were professors who, whenever a class ended, would bow deeply to the students. The gesture meant that they appreciated how we attended their classes to the very end. They did it after each class because they knew there was always at least one student heading to war the next day. Those were hard times for us, and we wanted to live the best life we could. Our school made that possible.

When the incident with my friend happened, one of the reasons I wrote the petition was because I wanted to repay our professors and our school for all they had done for us.

I liked philosophy. Before I died I wanted to read Kant's *Critique of Pure Reason* in the original German. I had never learned the language, but I studied as hard as I could and read the book, constantly referring to a dictionary.

I was only twenty, but I was sure I knew how to think for myself. As I majored in philosophy, I constantly thought about how people should live and die when the state conducted wars. I was a schoolboy when the Japanese military staged the Manchurian Incident that led to the Japanese invasion of China. For people my age, war was a constant in our lives, so we never asked why they happened in the first place.

In December 1944, I joined the Tottori Regiment. Two weeks later I was sent to China. There were not many of us in the frontline combat unit, and we assumed we would die.

We were ordered to the site of the Battle of West Henan in June of 1945. We took up a post on a plateau that was 1240 meters high. Visibility was good, but we knew the enemy would eventually overpower us; it was just a matter of time.

At dawn on June 11, a division of several thousand enemy troops attacked us all at once. The Allied forces had much more firepower than we did. We saw them arrive in a forest with trench mortars several hundred meters away, but after that I lost track of what was happening. The bullets began to fly. We shot back until our weapons were hot.

First I got shot in the right leg, but the next time I got shot, everything went white. My iron helmet was blown off, and I could feel my entire body fly through the air. It felt like I'd been hurled into a pot that was burning hot. I realized that I couldn't see. the *optical nerves in my brain were destroyed*, I thought, and surely no human could survive brain injuries.

I was alone; I couldn't hear a sound around me. I was the oldest of five boys, and my thoughts were on my family. I prayed that my younger brothers would be better sons to our parents than I had been. In my heart I said good-bye to each one of them.

I was ready to die and could feel the end coming. I wiped away my tears—and I could see! It wasn't my brain after all. I had a cut on my forehead that had bled so much it covered my eyes. The instant I realized what had happened, I was filled with an incredible energy. *I'm alive!* I wandered around until dawn, when another unit found me. My clothes were in tatters and my naked rear end was sticking out. There are still fragments of trench mortars in my right leg. You can see them on X-rays.

Most of my unit was killed in the battle. I had heard them screaming that they'd been shot, but there was nothing I could do. I still wish I could have helped them somehow. I know that it was impossible, but the trauma remains.

I wasn't able to return home after the war was over. Disarmament took place in November 1945, and after that I was sent to a POW camp in Zhengzhou. There I suffered from malaria and starvation. I was so malnourished that I dropped from sixty kilograms to less than forty.

In April 1946 I was finally repatriated via Senzaki Port in

Yamaguchi Prefecture. While I was on the ship waiting to come ashore, I read a newspaper that contained a draft of the new constitution. I couldn't believe it when I read Item 2 of Article 9,[1] which said, "The right of belligerency of the state will not be recognized." But then I read the same thing in another newspaper. I was astonished!

When the other men in my outfit read it, they all broke down in tears. While we'd been in prison, we'd talked about whether we could create a nation that would never go to war again. We'd agreed that if we couldn't, the souls of our comrades who had died in battle could never be consoled. The possibility of it being clearly codified in our constitution never crossed our minds. This was my first contact with the Japanese Constitution. I'll never forget it.

In the past I had assumed that the government would always wage war. When I went to war and saw it with my own eyes, though, I immediately started having doubts about why it was necessary.

Who are we fighting for? Even if Japan wins this war, will that make us truly happy, killing so many Chinese?

I finally realized that we shouldn't be at war, that the citizens of the countries involved had nothing against each other. When I thought about who and what we were fighting for, I came to understand that the war wasn't about anything as abstract as "the nation." None of it made sense until I found out that the real people who stood to profit from armed conflict were the Japanese Kwantung Army in Manchuria, the core members of the military, and the munitions industry. They were the ones who started it.

If human beings start wars, then human beings can stop them. That's what I learned as a soldier in combat. The men who served in the war as officers and were treated well went on to become leaders in politics and finance. But they never knew the misery of war. We soldiers were the ones who had to fight the battles.

The worst thing about combat was that individuality could not exist. Soldiers in battle were not allowed free will and merely had to obey orders. Losing my identity on the battlefield left me feeling empty after having spent so much time and effort pondering how to live as a human being.

After the war my mission in living was to reclaim my sense of purpose. If I had died on that 1240 meter-high plateau, I would never have been able to do anything for society. Thankfully I survived; and I am proud to say that I make the most of my life, saying things I feel I must say. Living is enormously rewarding if you can do that.

Human beings both cause wars and are able to prevent them. I understand that now as I watch the effort being made to alter the constitution. Who is trying to change the constitution and start wars? It's very clear who in Japan is responsible.

Politicians and financiers say they want to revise Article 9 because Japan and the US have common values. If we can declare that Japan, whose constitution forbids it to go to war, has completely different values from America, who is constantly at war supporting the military industrial complex, it would be even more revolutionary than tearing down the Berlin Wall.

If we can declare our pacifist intentions, we can change our relationships with other Asian countries that fear Japan will return to militarization. Even the US will have to change its strategy.

If Japan gets rid of Article 9 of the constitution, this doctrine of peace will disappear from the face of the earth. But in the twenty-first century, we need it now more than ever. The flag of our hopes and beliefs is in tatters right now, but if the Japanese choose to defend Article 9, it will fly higher than ever.

---

[1]Article 9—Aspiring sincerely to an international peace based on justice and order, the Japanese people forever renounce war as a sovereign right of the nation and the threat or use of force as means of settling international disputes. In order to accomplish the aim of the preceding paragraph, land, sea, and air forces, as well as other war potential, will never be maintained. The right of belligerency of the state will not be recognized.

Masaji Shinagawa Timeline

1924
Masaji is born on July 26 in the city of Kobe.

1931
Masaji, aged 7. The Manchurian Incident takes place.

1937
Masaji, aged 12. The Second Sino-Japanese War begins.

1941
Masaji, aged 17.
December: Japan invades the Malay Peninsula and attacks Pearl Harbor in Hawaii, beginning the Asia Pacific War.

1942
In June the Japanese navy suffers heavy losses in the Battle of Midway.

1944
At age 20, Masaji is drafted into the army on December 1 while still a student at Sanko High School.

1945
January: Masaji is sent to frontlines in China.
June: Masaji is wounded in battle.
Masaji, aged 21.
August 15: Japan accepts the Potsdam Declaration, defining the terms for Japan's surrender.
September: Masaji is sent to the POW camp in Zhengzhou City.

1946
April 30: Masaji repatriated to Japan by ship.

1949
March: Masaji graduates from Faculty of Law, the University of Tokyo. In 1984 he becomes CEO and chairman of present-day Sompo Japan Nipponkoa Insurance, chairman of International Development Center of Japan, and lifetime secretary of Japan Association of Corporate Executives.

August 29, 2013
Masaji dies at the age of 89.

Dear Shinagawa-san,

As I read your testimony, the first impression I had was that you and your best friend were very similar to me. Naturally the age we live in, and thus our worldview, is different. Still, I felt a kinship.

The only thing I know about the war is the Great Air Raid on Wakayama, which my grandfather told me about. Despite this lack of knowledge, I could not help feeling sympathy for you in your younger days, wavering between your experiences and your own thoughts formed through study, as well as for your friend who resisted in vain the trend of the times.

I felt the loss of my own individuality during my high school days, and I strongly rebelled against society. I read many philosophy books after entering university, although I never got as far as Kant's *Three Critiques*.

Like you, I also assumed that I had already formed my own thoughts. Even though we were not yet adults, a friend and I enthusiastically discussed the meanings of war and state. At that time I was pessimistic about human nature; I thought that war was the natural state of human beings. I believed that deterrence with nuclear weapons was the only way to maintain peace.

As you said, there is no doubt that the idea of Article 9 of the Constitution not only serves the general good; it is crucial. Unfortunately those of us who have lived only in peaceful times do not appreciate this.

The emptiness you experienced while on the brink of death and the misery of friends dying all around you. Regardless of the economic interests of a nation that goes to war, the battlefield is no more than the intensity of human emotions. Soldiers have parents; they have loved ones. How is it possible for them to fight and kill people against whom they hold no grudge? I cannot fathom it.

After I graduated from university, I saw friends trying to make their way in competitive, Japanese society, and I had one friend who committed suicide because he couldn't get along with others. In these situations I may have gotten a glimpse of the complicated feelings you experienced during and after the war.

I especially sympathized with these sentiments: *Who are we fighting for?* and *The worst thing about combat was that individuality could not exist.*

No doubt what I undergo in this era sounds quite trivial compared to what you went through on the battlefield.

I have shared some of my thoughts with you, and I believe that reading the reflections of your war experience has helped me to grow as an individual.

This letter has become one addressed to you in heaven, Shinagawa-san. I wish I could have spoken with you directly. I would like to have heard your stories in your own voice. Sadly that is impossible now, but I am resolved in following the example you have set, both as a leader in the business community of Japan and as a storyteller. I will carry your dreams for Article 9 in my heart so that I can raise high—along with the other members of my generation—the flag of our hopes and beliefs for the future of Japan.

With deep respect,
Naoto

Naoto Mitsume from Wakayama, Japan.
Age 27, graduate student in Tokyo.

Translation by Shota Kikuchi from Chiba, Japan.
Age 22, university student in Tokyo.

Shisono Hisamatsu
1924–2009
Treating A-bomb Victims in Nagasaki

"Living through the bomb was [my destiny].
That's why I feel I have to do whatever I can
whenever I am called upon."

At 11:02 AM on August 9, 1945. Just a few days after the US dropped the atomic bomb on Hiroshima, the next one exploded in Nagasaki. The wind and heat rays from the bomb destroyed the city in an instant. People living there died in agony and terror. At the time Shisono Hisamatsu was the head nurse of the physical rehabilitation department at Nagasaki Medical University. She lost many of the nurseswho worked under her. Despite their grief, she and her mentor, Doctor Takashi Nagai, treated the injured.

When the atomic bomb was dropped on Nagasaki, I was the head nurse in the physical rehabilitation department at Nagasaki Medical University.[1] I was head nurse, but I was only twenty-one years old.

That morning the air raid alarm had gone off but the all-clear had sounded, so we went back to our posts. A few nurses went outside to tend to our potato crop.

That's when it happened. There was a blinding flash of light followed by a huge explosion. The building I was in was made of concrete, but the ceiling came crashing down. I was too shocked to figure out what had happened. I struggled with all my might and finally managed to pull myself out of the rubble. My shoes had blown off my feet, and I couldn't find them anywhere.

I heard some other nurses calling me. I tried to reply, but my mouth was full of debris. The tap in the nurse's station had been blown open by the wind created by the bomb. I crawled over to it, washed my face twice, and gargled. I tried to wrap up some gauze bandages and other supplies in a piece of cloth and leave the room, but my hands were shaking too hard to tie it up.

Takashi Nagai[2] was a doctor in the physical therapy department. He was to later tell me—many times, in fact—that washing my face and gargling were the best things I could have done because it washed off the radiation. At the time, however, neither he nor I knew it was an atomic bomb. Many of the doctors and students at the school died that day.

I cremated the remains of five nurses by myself. They were the ones who had gone out to tend to the potatoes we'd planted on the school's athletic field, just below Urakami Cathedral,[3] a Catholic church that was also destroyed. I went out to look for the nurses the day after the bomb and found them burned black; their corpses had swollen grotesquely in the hot sunshine. Their hair stood on end. A few bits of colored cloth around their wrists and ankles was all that was left of their simple, wartime clothing.

I lined the bodies up and asked Dr. Nagai to light the fire. He said, "Absolutely not. You are the head nurse. These nurses work under you. Who but you should light the fire?" I was sad, so very sad.

"I'm sorry that I alone survived," I apologized to the dead girls as I lit the fire. The flames were high and they kept growing. I just stood there, staring at it.

Finally the doctor spoke, "Head Nurse, there are many injured people in the hospital waiting for us. We'll come back tonight to collect the bones of these women."

I obeyed. I had no other choice. In the school there was an endless stream of injured people. My white uniform was wet with the blood of the bomb victims who clung to me. There was no time to rest.

Dr. Nagai had been cut in the temple with a piece of glass; he was severely injured. He used the blood to paint the red sun of the Japanese flag on a piece of cloth.

"This is the school headquarters," he shouted out, "everybody gather here!"

Even before the bomb, Dr. Nagai had developed leukemia from the radiation he had absorbed from X-rays. He'd been told he had three years left to live. Now, on top of that, he had been irradiated by the bomb. The doctor's wife had died in the explosion, but he didn't stop to mourn; he took the lead in treating the wounded.

Sometimes he put his hand to his chest when he felt bad, or lied down for a little rest, but that was all. In my mind I can still see him at work.

On the third day after the bomb, I went with a rescue team to Mt. Mitsuyama, an area northeast of Urakami. Wounds became infested with maggots. To protect family members with open wounds, people put up mosquito nets to keep flies from laying eggs. We kept an eye out for the netting to help us identify people who needed help. While we were there, many people died in excruciating pain.

While I was away, my younger sister and brother had come to the hospital looking for me. They brought rice balls with them. Dr. Nagai greeted them saying, "Our head nurse is doing fine. It's dangerous here, so you go right back home!" He was a professional when it came to radiation exposure and knew how dangerous it was.

There are no words to express the state of Nagasaki after the bomb was dropped. The only people who can understand that tragedy are those who've experienced it. When I came back to the ruins of the hospital from Mitsuyama to stock up on medicine, I heard the radio broadcast of the Emperor announcing Japan's surrender.

I didn't feel relieved—I didn't feel anything but confusion. We had done more than we thought we were capable of to save people after the bomb because Japan was supposed to win the war. After all that we had gone through, we never expected Japan to lose. It took a while for me to just be happy that the war was over.

I got a bald spot on my head about the size of an egg. I became lethargic, and my adrenal glands were compromised. In the midst of the horror, I was sure I wouldn't live longer than few years. But I've passed the age of eighty! I'm thankful for every day that I have.

If meeting Dr. Nagai was part of my destiny, so was living through the bomb. That's why I feel I have to do whatever I can whenever I am called upon. You can't waste your life. Nurses must do their best to take care of their patients. They should always be beacons of light.

Once you're dead, there is no coming back. Life is more than acquiring material things. I learned this from Dr. Nagai. He did more to raise me than my own parents.

After the war, Dr. Nagai's health continued to decline. He lived out his remaining years together with his children in a tiny house he called Nyokodo. He always told them, "Even if you're left all on your own, you must oppose war." I gradually came to understand that we must never go to war again. Of course it took a while for me to feel that way.

I never married; I was always too busy to even consider it. Also, I was afraid that if I ever had children, they, too, would be affected by the radiation I had been exposed to. I worked as a nurse doing everything I could until I reached retirement. People have asked me if it was difficult to devote myself to helping others, but it wasn't.

Even now I still consult with Dr. Nagai and the historic, wartime nurse Florence Nightingale. I talk to them and ask for their advice before I fall asleep at night. And they always give me the answers I need. I can sleep well after they tell me I've done something right.

I visit the graves of my nurses who died. They are in Amakusa, Kumamoto, and Takashima. I always contact their families on the anniversary of the bombing and during the summer O-bon holiday. I believe it is my duty, both as the head nurse and as the one who survived.

That blinding light that dropped from the sky—I'll never forget it. Lightning is bright, right? Whenever lightning is forecast for the Nagasaki area, I close my storm doors. I'm still terribly scared of it.

[1] Nagasaki Medical University—The present-day Nagasaki University School of Medicine. Only 600 meters from the epicenter of the bomb, most of the school buildings were destroyed. More than 890 students, nurses, and instructors were killed in the blast.

[2] Takashi Nagai (1908–1951) —Dr. Nagai was a professor in the physical rehabilitation department at Nagasaki Medical University. Himself a victim of radiation exposure, he devoted the rest of his life to treating atomic bomb victims. He was a prolific author. The Bells of Nagasaki was published in English by Kodansha (1994) as a part of the Japan's Modern Writer series. His last years were spent with his children in a tiny, single-roomed home he called Nyokodo. The Nagai Takashi Memorial Museum Nagasaki was built next to it. It contains a record of the doctor's life and his messages calling for peace. http://nagaitakashi.nagasakipeace.jp/english/

[3] Urakami Cathedral—Work on the cathedral began in the late 19th century, and the church, made of brick, was completed in 1925. Only 500 meters from the bomb's epicenter, the cathedral was completely destroyed in the atomic bomb. Many members had come to pray and say confessions, and all present perished in the blast. A head of the statue of Mary, the mother of Christ, was found in the rubble of the cathedral. It has been nicknamed "Bombed Mary." Today the statue is kept in a small chapel in the rebuilt cathedral, where believers and tourists still flock to see it. The statue was part of an Atomic Bomb Exhibition taken to Vatican City in 1985.

Shisono Hisamatsu Timeline

1924
Shisono is born on January 15 in city of Nagasaki.

1941
At 17, Shisono begins work as a nurse at Nagasaki Medical University.
December: Japan invades the Malay Peninsula and attacks Pearl Harbor in Hawaii, beginning the Asia Pacific War.

1942
Shisono, aged 18. In June, the Japanese navy suffers heavy losses in the Battle of Midway.

1944
At the age of 21, Shisono becomes head nurse of the Physical Rehabilitation Department at Nagasaki Medical University.

1945
Shisono, aged 21.
August 6: The US drops the atomic bomb on Hiroshima.
August 9: An atomic bomb is dropped on Nagasaki.
August 15: Japan accepts the Potsdam Declaration, defining the terms for Japan's surrender.

1951
Shisono, aged 27. Her mentor, Dr. Takashi Nagai, dies.

1977
At 53, Shisono is appointed director of Nagasaki Medical University.

1985
At the age of 61, Shisono retires after 44 years as a nurse and is appointed Director Emeritus of Takashi Nagai Memorial International Hibakusha Medical Center.

2005
At 81, Shisono receives the 40th Florence Nightingale Medal.

January 8, 2009
Shisono dies at the age of 84.

Dear Shisono-san,

Hello, I am a sixteen-year-old freshman in high school.

When I was asked to write this letter, I hesitated a little. People need to know, however, that teenagers, and even young children, are experiencing war right now. This was my motivation.

After reading your story, I realized that you had gotten wounds in your heart that will never heal when you were as young as me, and still bravely went on living. I thought I should not write a casual letter to such a courageous person, so I write to you using the honorific "san" to express my respect.

We are a family of four. Until last year I lived with my father, mother, and younger brother. Now I am living with a family in Gunma prefecture and going to a high school near here. I have a lot of fun, but I feel down sometimes, too. When I talk to my family on the phone, they listen to me empathically and say, "that must be hard" or "I envy you your good experiences." Even though they are busy with household chores and work, they sometimes send me packages and tell me cheerfully about things that have happened to them. I really love and treasure my family. You and your nurses shared your lives and treated many patients together, so you undoubtedly felt like a family, too. You must have suffered a lot when you suddenly lost them and had to cremate their bodies yourself.

"It took me a while to be glad that the war was over." This is the sentence from your testimony that struck me the most and challenged my views.

When we learn about war in social studies classes in school, mostly they teach us about how wars started and ended, the number of people who died, and other facts like that. I have watched quite a lot of movies and dramas about the war as well. Most of the protagonists and their families say they long for the war to be over. So I automatically

assumed that people who actually lived during the war must have wanted it to be over. You taught me that it was not that simple. For those who strived so hard and sacrificed so much for the sake of Japan, it was unacceptable that our country had lost.

Today Japan is against war, and everyone thinks we should never repeat it. The fact that not everyone was immediately overjoyed that the war was over is something we young people might not understand. I would like to ask you, Shisono-san, when was the moment you started to be glad that the war was finally over?

A flash of lightening...it must be terrifying when a flash of lightening reminds you of the atomic bomb, and it is unbelievable to me that you have lived most of your life with that fear. I cannot imagine what it must have felt like with your mouth full of waste or what the dead nurses looked like. I have heard that things too horrible to contemplate can become everyday occurrences during wartime. I can only hope I will never find out.

I think the only thing we can do today is pass on the memories of the disaster and tragedy of war to children of the younger generation, just like you did for me.

Sincerely,
Ten

Ten Sugimura from Chiba, Japan.
Age 16, high-school student in Gunma.

Translation by Nozomi Kubota from Saitama, Japan.
Age 21, university student in Tokyo.

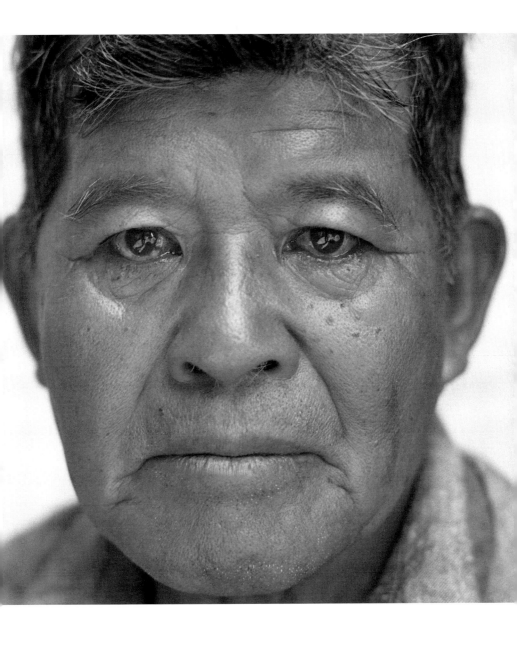

Zenko Nakasoko
1935–2016
Suffered from Malaria During Forced Evacuation

*"I won't forget how Shama was
beaten to death."*

*In April 1945 the Japanese army forced the entire population
of Hateruma, the southernmost inhabited island of Japan, to
evacuate to Iriomote Island and settle in a village that was
known as a breeding ground for Anopheles gambiae, also
known as the malaria mosquito. The village was available for
occupation because most of the former inhabitants had died
in a plague of malaria. The people of Hateruma knew this and
tried to object to living there, but they were powerless against
military orders. By the end of the war, five hundred of the
population of sixteen hundred died of what they referred to as
"war malaria."*

*The Hateruma population found out that their evacuation
had been ordered by Torao Yamashita, a graduate of the
Nakano Military Academy. They were placed under the control
of Yamashita and forced to cooperate with the war effort.
Zenko Nakasoko, nine years old at the time, had a friend who
Yamashita beat to death.*

*The people of Hateruma were told that the evacuation was
carried out to keep the invading Americans from taking over
the farm animals on the island and that the Japanese army was
seizing them as food for their soldiers.*

*When the islanders were getting ready to repatriate—minus
the hundreds who had died—the principal of their school,
Shinsho Shikina, admonished them to never forget the tragedy
of war malaria. A rock carved with simple characters that say
"Never-forget Rock, Hateruma, Shikina" still stands on the
Haemida coastline of Iriomote Island.*

I was nine years old and a fourth grader. The army sent an order that said, "Inhabitants of Hateruma Island must evacuate to Iriomote Island." The principal of the school, Mr. Shikina, and his wife, Kiyo, objected to it, saying Hateruma Island had caves and other places we could hide from the enemy. They didn't see any point in the evacuation.

The worst part of it was the malaria. Many years before, in the district of Haemida, where we'd been ordered to settle, there had been a village that was wiped out by the disease. We all knew about it. Nobody wanted to go to a terrible place like that.

Then a guy named Torao Yamashita,[1] an instructor from a military academy, appeared out of nowhere and pulled out his military sword.

"I'll kill anyone who turns his back on me!" he shouted at us. This Yamashita was tall, and I thought he was dashing the first time I saw him. But his personality changed as the war drew nearer.

We evacuated to Iriomote Island in April. I went along with fourteen of my relatives.

Before we left, my father covered the eyes of the five or six cows and pigs we owned and killed them with a hammer. This, too, was an order from the military. Everyone on the island got rid of their livestock. All of the meat was salted or smoked at the bonito plant. We got to keep a little, but the rest was confiscated by the army.

The group who went ahead of us had built evacuation shelters. We were divided up into groups and assigned to shelters. It was terribly hard on the adults, but community living was fun for us children. I wasn't homesick; I was with my family after all. I was sent into the fields to cut grass to thatch new shelters. I tied it on my back—just like you'd do to carry a baby. It was fun.

We weren't allowed to play on the beach during the day. They told us the enemy might see our footprints in the sand and know we were there. We had no freedom during those war years under the watchful eye of Yamashita.

Another job that fell to us children was to catch flies. Yamashita ordered us to do it because flies could spread disease. He gave us all bamboo tubes to use for that purpose.

One day Yamashita showed up and demanded we show him all the flies we had caught. Koyu Fusoko was a boy four years older than me—we all called him Shama (Big Brother). He only had a few flies in his tube. Yamashita made all of us line up and had Ishino, a young teacher who was assigned to do Yamashita's dirty work, beat all of us in turn with a bamboo pole. I'll never forget how badly that hurt.

Ishino saved the worst beating for Shama, hitting him over and over with a pole of green bamboo. Ishino didn't stop until the bamboo was in shreds. Shama tried to protect his rump with his hands, so Ishino beat him there.

At the time the adults were all out working. Only the older people were at home. There was no one to help us. Old Mrs. Onaka broke down in tears and put her hands together to beg for mercy.

"He doesn't deserve this!" she pleaded.

That night Shama broke out in a fever, and he died a few days later. He was a gentle boy who always played with me. He must have been in agony. I could never forgive what happened to him. And for what? Not catching enough flies!

Almost all of us got sent to malaria-filled Haemida, but the people who did things for Yamashita were evacuated to Yubu Island or safer parts of Iriomote, such as Komi. It wasn't fair.

When someone died on Hateruma Island, they were loaded onto a *gandara*, a platform like a portable shrine. We covered it in colored paper and said our good-byes. We didn't have anything, though, in Haemida. Shama was wrapped in a mat of woven plume grass and buried near a shelter. His mother was so sad.

After Shama died, old Mrs. Onaka ate some coconut crab and died of food poisoning.

Then the malaria began. It was what we had feared the most. People began to get sick, and the weakest—the children and the elderly—died of the disease.

I got malaria, too. It started with chills. I was so cold I shook. In less than an hour I had a fever. Someone cut a branch of a plantain for me to use as a pillow, and someone else poured water over my head. Pouring water was the job of anyone who didn't have malaria yet.

In August we finally got to go home to Hateruma Island, but it didn't stop the death. My father's younger brother dug a hole in the jungle near the sea and buried many people there. One entire family of sixteen people died, and there were others like it.

Lots of children died, so it was a while before school started again. All of our livestock had been destroyed, so we had nothing to eat except cycads. First they were boiled and then strained over and over until the concoction was a starchy flour. Finally it hardened into an edible gelatin—like substance. Many more people would have died if we hadn't had those plants.

Years later, when the war was over and I'd turned seventeen, I left Hateruma Island and came back to Iriomote as part of the Planned Immigration of the Government of the Ryukyus.[2]

People on Hateruma mocked me, asking if I was going back to die. But our island was so small. There was no land for second or third sons like me to start farms. I had to leave to get land of my own.

Back then I dreamed of becoming a sailor and seeing the world. Now that the war was over, I wanted to see what a world at peace looked like. It didn't work out, though. I cleared out the jungle to grow bananas and pineapple. I got a ship and used it to establish shipping routes between the islands of Iriomote and Ishigaki. I've been working this whole time. I like working. When I'm done for the day, food tastes good and so does sake.

I'll probably never go back to Hateruma. They laughed at me, so I swore never to go back, and I still feel that way.

I'll never forget what happened during the war. Being killed by a bomb is one thing. But the people of Hateruma were sent somewhere they didn't need to go, and then they died.

I won't forget how Shama was beaten to death. I'll never forgive that act. Not Yamashita and not Ishino either. War itself is unforgivable. If there hadn't been a war, we never would have been evacuated, and Shama would have lived. No one would have died of malaria.

---

[1] Torao Yamashita—The Nakano School, a military academy, trained spies during the war and sent some to the remote islands of Okinawa. One of them, a Sergeant Kiyoshi Sakai (age 25 at the time) took on the alias of Torao Yamashita and claimed to be an instructor. In January 1945 he was assigned to the national people's school on Hateruma Island. In March of the same year he forced the entire population off the island and sent them to Iriomote.

[2] Planned Immigration of the Government of the Ryukyus—This was a scheme developed after the war for people in Okinawa whose land had been seized for US military bases or who otherwise found it difficult to make a living. Immigrants were sent to remote Okinawa islands, or to Argentina, Brazil, Bolivia, and other South American countries.

Zenko Nakasoko Timeline

1935
Zenko is born on December 24 on Hateruma Island, Okinawa Prefecture.

1941
Zenko, aged 5.
December: Japan invades the Malay Peninsula and attacks Pearl Harbor in Hawaii, beginning the Asia Pacific War.

1944
Zenko, aged 8. On October 10 the US carries out an air raid on Okinawa.

1945
Zenko, aged 9.
April 1: The US forces land on the main island of Okinawa. The population of Hateruma Island is forced to begin a move to a malaria infested district of Iriomote Island where many die of "war malaria." Zenko's friend is beaten to death by a spy sent from the Nakano School, a military academy.
June 22: The Japanese army is defeated in the Battle of Okinawa.
August: The population of Hateruma returns home, although its inhabitants continue to die of malaria.
August 15: Japan accepts the Potsdam Declaration, defining the terms for Japan's surrender.

1951
Zenko, aged 15. The Treaty of San Francisco is signed in September. Okinawa is put under the administration of the US.

1953
At the age of 17, Zenko immigrates to Iriomote Island as a part of the Planned Immigration of the Government of the Ryukyus. He runs a banana and pineapple plantation and develops shipping routes between the islands of Iriomote and Ishigaki.

1972
Zenko, aged 36. On May 15, Okinawa reverts back to Japan.

March 17, 2016
Zenko dies at the age of 80.

Dear Zenko-san,

I very much appreciate you sharing your painful experiences. I had never before heard the story of what happened to the people of Hateruma Island during the war. I had heard that two hundred thousand people died in the Battle of Okinawa, but I could not believe that the imperial army cruelly plundered and murdered civilians to put off fighting on mainland Japan. You serve as an eyewitness that such brutal actions took place on islands other than mainland Okinawa.

Wars make humans inhumane. One-third of the residents of Hateruma Island died due to "war malaria," a disease they would not have gotten if they had not been forced off their island. It seems that wars not only cause physical damage, but also compassionless, ruthless behavior that results in countless lives being cut short.

I cannot imagine the distress the people of Hateruma felt when they were displaced from their homes by a senseless order and sent to an abandoned village swarming with malaria. The death of Shama, in particular, affected me deeply. He was killed while catching flies as ordered. I was saddened to learn that such violence took place among the Japanese people during the war.

I am currently working with children aged six to nine. So it is heartbreaking to think that you experienced war when you were as young as the children I work with now. You must have been an innocent and playful child. You must have enjoyed time with your family and friends. The war stole so much of your precious childhood. When I learned that the loss of Shama still haunts you, I realized that the wounds of war continue to deepen long after the war is over.

There are wars happening right now all over the world, and I want to stop them as soon as possible. We need to learn from the past and think about the kind of future we want to see in Japan. Seventy years have passed since the end of the war. We have little time left to listen

to the voices of war survivors. It is my duty, as a member of the post-war generation, to listen to as many witnesses as possible and to remember and share their thoughts and stories with as many people as possible. I promise to work with others to pass on a peaceful society to the next generation.

Sincerely,
Natsuki Hatae

Natsuki Hatae from Fukuoka, Japan.
Aged 24, company employee in Tokyo.

Translation by Hajime Akiyama from Tokyo, Japan.
Age 26, graduate student in Tokyo.

Photographer's Notes:
Portraits of the Energy of Life

Yuriko Ochiai

As a photographer, I am often confronted with the poverty of my imagination concerning things I haven't bothered to learn about. One example is the time I went to Okinawa to meet war survivors.

I learned a little about the land war and forced mass suicides on the main Okinawan island and the nearby Kerama archipelago. Satisfied with what I now knew, I began to think about the many islands further south that are a part of Okinawa prefecture. How did the people living there spend the war years? *Maybe they managed to avoid it altogether and lived in relative peace*, I thought.

With this optimistic image in my mind, I decided to go meet some of the residents of this remote part of Japan. It wasn't long before I learned how wrong I was.

Hateruma Island is the southernmost inhabited island of Japan. In April 1945 the population of the entire island, including Zenko Nakasoko, was forced to evacuate to nearby Iriomote Island. They were sent to live in a district well-known for its malaria-carrying mosquitoes. Just as the evacuees feared, many contracted the disease and a third of the Hateruma natives died of what they dubbed "war malaria."

It's impossible to know everything, I concluded, but I can learn about what happened, one event at a time. And I can listen carefully to what those who lived through the war have to say. Their experiences were significant and miserable, things happened that I could never have imagined. The amazing part was that learning those stories gave me courage to keep on living.

I looked at each of my subjects and savored the unique nature of our meeting with each picture I took, and I hope that readers who see these photographs feel the same way.

Several years later I began taking photos of the letter writers, all in their teens and twenties. The tide of Japan's peaceful existence no longer seemed as certain as it had when I was making the portraits of the survivors.

Even after receiving the letters written by young people to the war survivors, I was having trouble deciding how I should portray them. The answer came to me right before it was time to start the shoots. "Give me four hours," I requested of each subject. "Let's walk around together in a place you like and where you feel relaxed, and I'll take photographs of you along the way."

And that's what happened. As we walked, I listened to what the young person I was with that day had to say. When the moment was right, I stopped and took a picture.

On one particular day, as my time with one subject came to a close, we sat down together on a river embankment.

"I don't know," the youth began, "war might have been easier than what I went through. No bombs fell, but there wasn't any peace for me…" There was hesitancy in the words, but as I listened, bits and pieces of the conversation we'd had throughout the day suddenly came together, and I felt the weight of everything this young person had experienced.

Yasuji Kaneko, whose story is told in this book, has been an anti-war activist, telling people about the violent acts he committed as a soldier, and insisting that a situation in which such acts are possible must never again be repeated.

I remembered the day I was taking his picture. I asked him what he would say to a young person who was tired of living. This is what he said:

"It's not that I don't understand the feeling. But I've seen lots of people die, and I can tell you that living is more precious."

The young person I was with that day went on to tell me that writing the letter for this book turned out to be a new beginning for him. I nodded, sure that it had been the same for all of the youthful writers. As I finished taking the photographs, I realized it was the same for me, too. This was my new beginning.

p.8–9 : Nishihama Beach, Haterumajima Island, Okinawa
p.200–201 : Haterumajima Island, Okinawa
p.202–203 : Hiroshima
p.204–205 : Tenma River, Hiroshima
p.206–207 : The camphor tree of Sanno Shrine in Nagasaki that survived the atomic bomb
p.208 : In the hands of a former Japanese soldier

Afterword:
An appeal for peace sent out into the world

Naomi Kitagawa

The Japanese Constitution is often affectionately and proudly referred to as the "peace constitution" because it prohibits Japan from ever going to war again. There is movement, however, to change the constitution and the shape of the nation into one that can go back to war. This alarming push has grown in leaps and bounds since this book was first published in Japanese in 2015.

Yumiko Sakuma is a prominent translator of children's books and a witness to worldwide cultural shifts through the literature she works with. In a note of support for the English translation of this book, Sakuma told us how distressed she is to see an increase in the number of people who value "money over life" and "follow-the-leader behavior over diversity." To return value to the life of each individual, she believes, we must understand war and who benefits from it. Now is the time, she states, for people from all over the world to read this book, with its focus on life and diversity, and to think long and hard about the meaning of life.

Four years have passed since the publication of *1945←2015: Reflections on Stolen Youth* originally published under the title *Letters from Young People to Young People: 1945←2015*. Four years may not seem that long, but during those years we lost many of the fifteen war survivors whose stories are published here. Only three are still alive. Soon after publishing the book, we realized that the same was true of survivors of World War II in all countries. As there are fewer alive who remember that time, the memories are fading globally. Maybe the stories of this horrific war and our fervent desire that it never be repeated needed to be communicated to other people and in other languages. And so we started a project to translate this book into English and spread it throughout the world. We were encouraged to do so by people we know who have introduced Japanese books abroad as well as friends working in international NGOs. What started out as a dream has turned into reality, and we are excited to find out how people throughout the world receive this book.

The stories of the war survivors have been translated by Deborah Iwabuchi, an American who has translated the works of numerous popular Japanese writers. She accepted our request to take on this project because she felt it was important. The translation was carried out thoughtfully as we all read and re-read each story in both languages. We authors provided background as needed, and many times we worked through cultural differences and discussed the accuracy and suitability of single words and phrases to make sure the full intention of our wartime witnesses was communicated. Despite the past relationship of Japan and the US, in this book, Iwabuchi joined us in our commitment to this plea for peace.

To translate the letters of young people to our war survivors, we chose translators of the same age range. We were fortunate to find youth from many different countries—South Korea, China, the Philippines, Singapore, Senegal, and Peru, as well as Japan—who could read and write both Japanese and English. We imagine that the grandparents of these different translators experienced the war and would have thought of each other as enemies, but here are their grandchildren working together for peace. We authors discovered new hope and energy in this collective effort. Out of the original project came presentations by these young people at their school festivals and peace-related events put on by municipalities. We were surprised to find out that plans are in the making to get the original letter writers and translators together. We are certain that all of these activities are and will be steps toward a lasting world peace. The next step in this project will be encouraging these young people to help us achieve our goal of a global discussion about war and peace. Using this book as an opportunity to do so, we are beginning to see young people reaching out toward others of their generation.

Finally, the English version of this book is being sent out into the world thanks to all of the people who supported us in crowdfunding. We were surprised and delighted to find out just how many people agreed with the deep desire for peace of our war survivors and letter writers. Please take a look at the back of the book to find the names of all our crowdfunding contributors.

Nothing could possibly be better than for this book to serve as an opportunity to bring people of the world together and begin a conversation about doing away with war. I would like to offer my deepest appreciation to all the people who shared our dream, contributed to this project, and helped in the production of this book.

Translator's Notes

Deborah Iwabuchi

I was born in the US during the post-World War II baby boom to a family of closely spaced generations who all avoided the draft by virtue of being a little too young or a little too old. Everything I knew about the war was gleaned from the printed page. I am one-quarter ethnic Jew, and I lapped up books with Jewish themes that often began or ended with the Holocaust. The Pacific War was not on my radar except for textbook mentions of the atomic bombs and Pearl Harbor.

Fate, however, led my attention away from the European continent and straight to Japan. My first trip was in 1973, a clueless seventeen-year-old American looking for adventure. The first stop on my itinerary was Hiroshima, where I took classes in Japanese.

At the end of two weeks, I spent two nights with a middle-aged couple and their thirty-year-old son. The son was eager to practice his limited English on me and I (still) had no Japanese to speak of. After he had asked me every personal question he was linguistically capable of, I decided to return the favor, asking him whether he had any brothers or sisters.

"Brother," he said.

"Where is he now?" I asked.

"The bomb," he said, with an uncomfortable expression.

"Oh," I replied, and we went on to another topic.

Almost thirty years after the atomic bombs had been dropped on Hiroshima and Nagasaki, it was perhaps still too delicate a subject to broach. Forty years since that meeting, after reading the stories of Sanae Ikeda, Hiroko Iwami, and Shisono Hisamatsu, I want to know where that young man, his brother, and his parents were when the bomb was dropped on Hiroshima. What had meant the difference

215

between life and death in that particular family? And what had moved them past their grief enough to be able to open up their home to me?

Some of the other stories in 1945←2015 have connections to my sadly inadequate knowledge of the war, and I treasure those connections, but even more so the countless other details that I learned here for the first time. The fifteen survivors have become my heroes, and it has been an honor for me to be entrusted with the translation of their stories into English.

Motomi Murota and Naomi Kitagawa who conducted and compiled interviews and invited letters from young people, were passionate, patient, and exacting. They provided me with background not included in the stories to make sure the interpretations were properly grounded. Both of these women, it should be noted, have conducted the entire project by building relationships with each person involved—not just the fifteen war survivors, but the fifteen young people who wrote letters to the survivors, and the fifteen more who translated them into English. Murota and Kitagawa brought in Manami Yasuda, a book designer, who has done an amazing job of creating a book as attractive and inviting as any publication could possibly be. Together with Yuriko Ochiai, the book's photographer, and Takayoshi Kise of Korocolor Publishers, the authors also managed to generate enthusiasm for the English version of this book and finance it through crowdfunding here in Japan, acknowledging their appreciation for each and every donation. Translation is a quiet, solitary sort of occupation. I have never worked on a project for which there was so much activity besides the actual translation work. To describe the commitment devoted to the English version of 1945← 2015 as a "labor of love" would be an understatement.

My enduring thanks goes to Stephanie Umeda, my New York–based editor, who graciously agreed to take on this project even before the crowdfunding came into the picture. Stephanie has done a wonderful job of smoothing out the wrinkles and bringing the stories and letters to life. It's not often that I have such great backup—people tend to think a translator alone is good enough to get the whole job done, but no, it's not true. The translator gets so attached to and mired in the original—especially when the topic is so gut-wrenching. It takes a top-notch editor to recognize the pain, emotion, and conviction, and make sure the readers experience it, too.

Finally, let me say that this project—the fifteen survivor stories in their entirety—has taught me much more than the heartbreaking specifics of one particular war. The first thing I learned was how many different ways war can be horrible. If you read the book, you'll know what I mean.

It was also interesting to note that, despite the different experiences of these survivors and how they suffered, as well as how some of them caused suffering themselves, they all independently came to the same conclusion: there is no justifiable reason to wage war.

The survivors lived through hell, clawed their way back toward life, and then had decades to sort through their experiences. The observations they make here at the end of their long and complicated lives are laid out simply, gifts for us to cherish, lessons to be learned and passed on.

As survivor Yoshio Shinozuka put it, "War is ruthless and indiscriminate, so I believe we should not go to war or have an army... *What need do we have to destroy peace?*"

Learning More at Museums

Below is a list of museums where readers can learn more about Japan and the Asia Pacific War (websites have English versions unless otherwise noted).

[*Included is the name of the war survivor in this book connected with the subject matter of the museum.*]
All museum information is current as of March 2020.

Atomic bomb

Nagasaki Atomic Bomb Museum [*Sanae Ikeda*]
https://nagasakipeace.jp/english/abm.html

Nagai Takashi Memorial Museum Nagasaki [*Shisono Hisamatsu*]
http://nagaitakashi.nagasakipeace.jp/english/

Hiroshima Peace Memorial Museum [*Hiroko Iwami*]
http://hpmmuseum.jp/?lang=eng

Maruki Gallery For The Hiroshima Panels
http://www.aya.or.jp/~marukimsn/english/indexE.htm

Air raids

The Center of the Tokyo Raids and War Damage [*Michiko Kiyo-oka*]
http://www.tokyo-sensai.net/old/english_page/index.html

Grass Roots House Peace Museum
https://ha1.seikyou.ne.jp/home/Shigeo.Nishimori/english/

Evacuated children

Tsushima-maru Memorial Museum
http://tsushimamaru.or.jp/?page_id=85

Battle of Okinawa

Okinawa Prefectural Peace Memorial Museum
[*Michiko Miyagi, Koyu Kinjo, and Taeko Shimabukuro*]
http://www.peace-museum.pref.okinawa.jp/english/index.html

The Cornerstone of Peace, Peace Memorial Park
http://sp.heiwa-irei-okinawa.jp/stone/stone.html

Himeyuri Peace Museum
http://www.himeyuri.or.jp/EN/info.html

Yaeyama Peace Memorial Museum [*Zenko Nakasoko*]
https://www.pref.okinawa.jp/yaeyama-peace-museum/toukannitu-ite/leaflet_eng.pdf

Manchuria Pioneers

The Memorial Museum for Agricultural Emigrants to Manchuria [*Nobuko Yamatani*]
https://www.manmoukinenkan.com/english/

Sino-Japanese War

Chukiren Peace Museum Japan [*Yasuji Kaneko and Yoshio Shinozuka*]
https://npo-chuukiren.jimdo.com/
(Museum website is in Japanese, but a pamphlet is available in English.)

Former Site of Fushun War Criminals Management Center
[*Yasuji Kaneko and Yoshio Shinozuka*]
(Website is in Chinese only, but museum displays include explanations in English.)

Other

The defunct Imperial Japanese Army Noborito Laboratory Museum for Education in Peace
http://www.meiji.ac.jp/cip/english/institute/noborito.html

Women's Active Museum on War and Peace
https://wam-peace.org/en/

The Changi Museum [*Lee Hak Rae*]
http://www.changimuseum.sg

War in general

Kyoto Museum for World Peace, Ritsumeikan University
http://www.ritsumei.ac.jp/mng/er/wp-museum/english/index.html

Supporters of
1945←2015: Reflections on Stolen Youth

Many thanks to the following people who in many different ways generously supported publication of the English version of this book.

Hisae Sawachi
Yumiko Sakuma
Chen Tien-shi
Atsuko Hayakawa
Tsuda University
• Peace-Art Project,
• Translation
  Seminar, English
  Department
Masaru Tonomura
Nanako Inaba
Mitsuyoshi Himeta
Aiko Utsumi
Masaie Ishihara
Hironori Yamatani
Nanako Yashiro
Tadahito Yamamoto
Asami Ohmoto
Takeshi Kagoshima
Hiroyuki Ogawara
Ryuji Ishida
Aki Misawa
Aiko Kashimura
Yukinori Okamura
Fumiko Ishioka
Junpei Sekiguchi
Hiroto Oka
Toshimi Oka
Tomoaki Kageyama
Mieko Imao
Keisuke Imao
Chikara Yamada

Haruyo Kitagawa
Akiko Hirai
Hiroe Kawashima
Keunho Park
Toshihiko Ando
Toshitaka Tasaki
Hatsue Yoshimura
Shinobu Yoshimura
Hisae Orui
Chieko Murota
Nazuna Isa
Taro Urakawa
Hideyo Nakanishi
Ritsuko Saito
Katsuhiko Saito
Hisami Azegami
Yasuhisa Takemura
Mayuko Murata
Yui Osakabe
Keiko Yasuda
Kazufumi Yamaji
Ikuko Nishida
Megumi Nakajima
Yuki Ito
Sigeru Aoki
Suzuko Nakano
Miyako Yoshinaga
Yuko Kubota
Yukari Shimada
Shoko Aizawa
Kyoko Okazaki
Hiroshi Watanabe

HAIR en
Hiroko Miki
Mamiko Iwasaki
Nami Okubo
Sawako Homma
Masami Aoki
Chiyoko Miyakawa
Sari Komazaki
Tamaki Tago
Eiji Iidaka
Hiroko Iidaka
Hiroshi Iidaka
Kazuko Otsu
Yukari Numazaki
Yuko Adachi
Shiro Egawa
Jeong-suk Jo
Kazuhiro Imamura
Naoko
  Takahashi-Ando
Junya Tada
Masakazu Fukuhara
Masayo Yokoyama
Tokusaburo Nagai
Takahiro Sha
Takashi Fujimoto
Sachiko
  Tanaka-Morris
Mariko Nakasone
Tsugue Tanaka
Naoko Kitami
Norio Akashi

Hiroshi Hasegawa
Asumi Hayashi
Chikako Yagawa
Satoko
  Oka-Norimatsu
Sugimura Family
Masayuki Yagi
Yangja Suh
Mari Fujioka
Satsuki Shimizu
Takako Takahashi
Atsuko Ueda
Miki Shinada
Yuko Takiguchi
Hisako Matsui
Izumi Iwase
Miyuki Endo
Kikuno Murota
Hideyuki Takaoka
Mitoko Takaoka
Takeshi Nakatani
Masako Minaki
Maki Tateyama
Mariko Sakurai
Akiko Umezawa
Naoko Ataka
Michiko Miura
Masayuki Abe
Hiroyuki Watanabe
Shigeru Ozaki
Michiyo Tamai
Rieko Ashizawa

*There are others who wish to remain anonymous.

Jun Sasamoto
Mayumi Saito
Mie Kobayashi
Mitsue Kobayashi
Yoko Shima
Ryosuke Oshiro
Yosuke Watanabe
Keiko Matsumoto
Kaori Ichimura
Haruko Noda
Yoshiko Kawakami
Kumiko Oga
Miki Seta
Setsuko Noguchi
Maiko Sugamoto
Birei Ga
Setsuyo Nakanozaki
Michie Yamamori
Yukiko Kuroda
Junko Toyoda
Madoka Ogawa
Yoko Takanashi
Yuma Ohkuma
Moon Yong-Ae
Hitomi Nakazato
Andrew Wong
Kayo Azuma
Chieko Hirakata
Mitsuka Tokumoto
Rikako Taguchi
Shino Arisawa
Makiko Endo

Hiroshi Ishida
Mai Nakanishi
Miyuki Ogino
Keiko Yasuda
Masako Tsuchiya
Yuko Takabe
Tetsuya Amano
Yukie Iimuro
Kazue Shibasaki
Masahiro Inoue
Yukio Yoshimoto
Nobuko Komatsu
Keiko Yamasawa
Yasuo Tsuneoka
Taro Abe
Yoshiko Hayashi
Fumiko Kimura
Keiko Koutsusa
Momoko Kasuta
Tsukushi Yoshimura
Naoko Morinaga
Kumiko Kamei
Akiyo Uozumi
Hiroko Seki
Yoko Nadamitsu
Toshihide Nukaga
Masashi Ochiai
Yoshio Takeuchi
Kunio Kitame
Michihiko Oikawa
Sachiko Kato
Daiji Mori

Atsuko Omiya
Sawako Iwatsuki
Minori Okuda
Junko Kurihara
Takako Oe
Mitsuyo Kusaka
Kimiyo Muramoto
Akemi Yamazaki
Kuniko Tanoue
Yuichi Hida
Masako Tanoue
Akiko Yamamoto
Masao Sato
Michiko Chiba
Mariko Ichikawa
Akio Ito
Setsuko Kawai
Susumu Shirai
Makoto Sakaino
Hiroko Osono
Keiko Kurakam
Saeko Kanda
Kazuko Kamakura
Michiko Kikuchi
Wataru Horigome
Kuniko Mochimaru
Kaori Sakuma
Toshio Hori
Yoshiko Hosoda
Rie Yasui
Junko Higuchi
Miyoshi Itoh

Momoko Hirayama
Yukiko Hagiwara
Michiyo Arakawa
Hiroshi Hori
Nobuo Serizawa
Atsuko Akiyama
Koji Sugihara
Akira Kawanabe
Reiko Ashizawa
Yukio Oka
Miyuki Oka
Toshie Kitame
Sadamu Yamagata
Masaki Tsutsumi
Yohei Achira
Masashi Haga
Kazuho Niwa
Chieko Seki
Hibiki Yoshimura
Chunzhi Li
Longzhi Li
Mingzhe Li
Izumi Beatrice
Imamura

About the Authors, Photographer, and Translator

Motomi Murota, author

Born in 1960, she began her career as a magazine writer and FM radio broadcast writer. She now writes and reports mainly on topics related to the Asian Pacific War and the history of East Asia. Books include (titles translated from the Japanese) *Archipelago of Grief: That Day Somewhere in Japan* (Shakaihyoronsha, 2010), which won the Incentive Prize in the 16th Peace & Cooperative Journalist Awards, *What I Want to Say Now: Talking to East Asian Youth About History* (Kodomonomiraisha, 2014), and *Memories of the Land: Scars From the War Continue to Speak* (Shakaihyoronsha, 2018).

Naomi Kitagawa, author

Born in 1960, she earned a Master of International Affairs degree from the University of Tsukuba Graduate School. She has served as chief editor of *Winds*, the JAL in-flight magazine, and *Spring Board*, published by the Japan Overseas Cooperative Association. Her books published as a freelance editor have all had themes of recording and preserving wartime memories, including (titles translated from the Japanese) *Refugees and Landmines* (Soudobunka, 2002), *Germany Clinging to Memories* and *New Challenges for the World's Only "Peace Constitution"* (both Otsuki Shoten Publishers, 2012 and 2010), *What I Want to Say Now: Talking to East Asian Youth About History* and *Walking Among Memories of the Holocaust* (both Kodomonomiraisha, 2014 and 2016), and others.

Yuriko Ochiai, photographer

She was born in 1963 and graduated from Nihon University College of Art. She received a college award for her graduation work *Window's Whisper*. She documented people in Eastern Europe and farming villages in Romania from 1989 through 1992 after the Berlin Wall came down. Her artistic policy is to spend time with her subjects and live their stories with them before taking their portraits. Her exhibits include *The Story of a Japanese Romanian* and *Working and Nurturing*, among others. Publications include (titles translated from the Japanese) *Grandma Kinu and the 90-year Journey: Her Memories of Living in Manchuria* (Kodansha, 2005), *Working and Nurturing* (Soudobunka, 2001), and *The Life of Hideko and Shuichi Tsubata* (Shizenshokutsushinsha, 2012, Bungeishunju, 2018), which was published internationally.

Deborah Iwabuchi, translator

Born in California in 1956, she first came to Japan in 1973 as a high-school student. After studying Japanese at the University of the Pacific, she came back to Japan as a missionary associate. She has been writing and translating since 1988, including works by such well-known Japanese authors as Miyuki Miyabe, Nobuko Takagi, Jun'ichi Watanabe, and Tomihiro Hoshino. She lives in Maebashi with her husband, Ikuo, runs Minamimuki Translations, Ltd., and teaches at Gunma Prefectural Women's University.

You are invited to write your own letter.

Send us your thoughts on
1945←2015: Reflections on Stolen Youth

We would be delighted to hear your impressions after reading the stories and letters in this book, and we invite readers around the world to send letters to the war survivors and young letter writers.

Today, conflicts over ethnicity, religion, and territory continue around the world. We hope that this book can transcend boundaries and serve as an opportunity for discussing why wars happen and how we can bring about peace.

We look forward to hearing from you! Send your letter to our publisher in Japan; please include: your name, age, occupation, city and country, and email address.

Letters received will be posted on our website:
https://1945-2015-letter.jimdofree.com
Send letters by email to: **tegami@korocolor.com**
Send letters by post to: **Korocolor Publishers**
Attn.: Korocolor editorial department
1-19-7-603 Akabane, Kita-ku, Tokyo, Japan
115-0045
http://korocolor.com/